Pearls of a Fisherman:
Lessons for the Mystical Life

Other books by this author:

The Word Within

The Radical Path

Spiritual Astrology

Steps on the Way

The Way, the Truth and the Life:
The Autobiography of a Christian Master

Father Peter Bowes

Pearls of a Fisherman:
Lessons for the Mystical Life

Sophia Publishing

Boston • Chicago • Milwaukee

Pearls of a Fisherman: Lessons for the Mystical Life

1st Edition
© 2011 Sophia Publishing
All rights reserved.
Printed in the United States of America

All citations of Poem of the Man-God provided with permission from:
Centro Editoriale Valtortiano
I 03036 Isola del Liri (Fr) – Italia
Tel. +39 0776 807 032 – Fax +39 07776 809 789
www.mariavaltorta.com
cev@mariavaltorta.com

For information, write to:
Sophia Publishing
1841 North Prospect Avenue
Milwaukee WI 53202

Contact Father Peter with any questions and
listen to podcasts of his teachings at:

www.FatherPeterBowes.com
www.CentersOfLight.org

Cover Art:
Reverend Meira Leonard and Grace Tenner

CONTENTS

∞

You can't serve God and the world.

The world will chew you up and spit you out.

The disciple is taught through love.

Love is the teacher,

compassion the instruction

and healing is the result.

– FATHER PETER BOWES

Chapter One

Are You Tired of Doing Things Your Way?

A re you tired of doing things your way? Are you aware that everything that happens to you was created by you? Have you ever thought about this? Your thoughts create everything in your life. When you think a thought, energy moves from within your mind, fueled by the feelings in your heart, and moves out into creation. We create the same way God creates as we are made in the spiritual likeness of God. When we want something, energy from our feelings and decision congeal around our desire. In this way, the thought takes on life and moves the energy of the universe to make happen what we decide. Each thought has a life of its own and will produce a result. The energy of our decision and wanting will make the difference in a thought that sluggishly manifests or one that dynamically manifests. How much you put your heart into your thinking determines how strongly the thought manifests.

This is the law of cause and effect, which is installed in the fabric of creation, perfectly wired to your wishes and desires to bring to you whatever you decide. Your thought goes into the mind of God and God brings it back to you in the form you imagined. Since you create everything that happens to you, how can you sit there and blame God for the conditions in your life? Is God responsible because you expressed a desire, want, wish, or demand on the universe and then the powers of the universe brought you the result of that desire, want, wish, or demand? Just because you forgot one of your silent thoughts or secret wishes, does not make anyone else responsible for them. You created them. You get to live with them.

When the law of cause and effect eventually brings you the results of your prayer or wish, you are surprised and even suffer a little amnesia about how this could have come about. If what you are experiencing is a negative thing, or if your desire was selfish and did not manifest quickly, you feel that somehow God has dealt you a fateful blow and you get upset. You would rather blame God than take responsibility for the fact that you put out that wish or prayer a long time ago and now it is at your door. You created it even though you have long since forgotten that you did. In the heat of one of your fits you spoke some things or thought some things and God's energy and intelligence registered your request. Since it was not that powerful of a to you. When it arrives, you become devastated and angry because life is so unfair. Why do bad things have to happen to a good person like you? What is God thinking that you have to be treated so unfairly and so unkindly?

If you are going to grow up to be a spiritual adult, you have to start taking responsibility for what you create. Everything that happens to you can only happen if you are open to it or actually request it. Some really bad things that happen to you may be the result of karma. In other words, you might have created the very thing you are experiencing now. Or, at times you may not have been actively making sure you were safe and protected from bad things happening to you. That means you were not taking precautions in your behavior to make sure you were safe. This concept probably makes you reflect on why major calamities and disasters happen to people. There are no accidents. This doesn't mean you should blame anyone. The point is that the universe is ordered. God is order. Life has intelligence that God placed into it and nothing happens by accident. Everything has a cause and even if you don't see the cause because of your limited vision it doesn't mean there isn't one. Everything has a cause if you have eyes to see what it is. Nothing can happen that does not have some seen or unseen cause behind it. The universe would be chaos if this was not the case. The people that like to believe the universe is chaos are trying to convince people that there is no great intelligence running things. They are mostly materialists who do not believe in God much less see the entire creation animated by the great being of the Creator. They are spiritually blind and only see what their physical eyes see. You should pay no attention to such people.

If you realize that your feeling and thinking are causing the things you are experiencing in your life, then it stands to reason that you would want to take some control of the process. I am sure you dislike being shocked and surprised by events. You are dismayed by catastrophes and disasters just like everyone else. I imagine you would want to be informed if something like that was coming your way, wouldn't you? Getting to know how God works and how God created this universe is the only way to prevent surprises from happening in your life. You need to know how God created this world if you are going to learn how to navigate its waters. Only if you steer your own ship can you make sure the things that happen to you are the things you actually want to happen. You have to take charge. Now, not everyone wants to be in charge. Not everyone wants to be responsible for everything that happens in life. But it is kind of a joke, because you already are. You have been in charge of everything that has ever happened to you. That means you have created things just the way you wanted them to be. Do you like what you have? Do you enjoy what you have built? Do you like what you have created?

If you do, then you are doing very well. If you don't, then change it. Make things the way you want them to be. Stop acting like little children who want everyone else to take responsibility for you. Cut out the tendency to ignore things or pretend that you have nothing to do with what happens.

Take responsibility. You definitely create your future by your present thinking and feeling. There are very few people who want to stop blaming others for their predicament. There are few who desire to stand up and be counted as someone who takes charge of his or her life and make his or her life what they want it to be. There are few these days who consciously control themselves to the extent of sacrificing their small, tiny egos for the benefits of a spiritual life. Taking conscious control of your emotions, thinking and desires is a daunting task. But it is vitally necessary to begin to climb the obstacle of the physical body and its emotions if you are ever to gain mastery over your future and the results of your thinking. You can definitely guide your future by being conscious in the present.

What is consciousness? What does it take to be conscious? Consciousness is a state of wakefulness in mind and feeling. It means you are open to the experience that is in front of you and inside you. It means being concentrated in the moment and holding the presence of the moment without trying to get away from it. If you are trying to rush through life or trying to get away from your thoughts, your body or your feelings, then you are not conscious in the present moment. Consciousness is God being aware of God's Self. God is the source of all consciousness, so we have consciousness to the extent that we are aware of God seeing, hearing and feeling through us. If you are cut off from God or God is not in the picture, your consciousness is limited indeed.

People spend most of their energy trying to get away from things that bother them. They glance over things in a shallow and hasty manner in order not to notice them or to avoid them. They often don't look closely at things or study energy or interactions long enough to learn from them. I suggest that you start watching energy. That means to pay attention to how energy is moving between two people. What is someone's energy trying to accomplish and what is their energy trying to do? You have to love things enough to spend time looking at them in order for those things to teach you something. It is just the same with another person. You have to pay attention to them in order to be interested in them. Paying attention to someone is loving them and accepting them enough to get to know them. This is what God does, this is consciousness. Consciousness is paying attention to your experience, paying attention to people around you and paying attention to your whole being. Not seeing, not wanting to know and shutting down your feelings so you don't have to feel them is an act of unconsciousness. When you don't focus your attention on what is happening inside you and around you, you have abdicated conscious control over your universe. You have become a ship in a storm-tossed sea, shoved around by every wind of emotion and every random thought. In this turbulence there is no peace. There can't be. That is the way most people live and they seem content to never question this experience.

If you already recognize that your mind is creating your life, you are probably tired of your mind or tired of your emotional reactions. Every day I hear people say they want to be free of confusion in thinking and feeling. They complain of the damage they are doing in their relationships, yet continue day after day to ravage themselves or others with the same old patterns. If you recognize yourself doing this, I suggest using your masculine energy: your ability to decide and state your objective to never think like that again, or never react emotionally like that again. It takes getting intensely disgusted with the way you have been to really want to change and stop the behavior. When you see that it hurts you and everyone else around you, you will stop it. Just cut it out and delete it from your vocabulary. If you persist and are determined, your body, mind and emotions will comply with your new wish and your new way of behaving.

When you actually try to do this, a part of you may rebel, or even defy you if you try to force it to stop. The problem for most people is that they are not used to that kind of discipline. You may have so seldom told yourself what to do that you go into shock to even think it is possible that you could be successful in complying with your own wish. When you allow yourself to get especially negative, many of you sit passive, shocked and bewildered at what is happening to you, and you just watch, stunned and intoxicated by how intense the energy is. At those times, when the negative energy takes you down, you don't question. You don't fight. You don't overcome the sludge of the onslaught of emotion or lack of it. You just stay emotionally numb or anesthetized. At those times, try going directly to prayer. Mother Mary is especially powerful at lifting us out of negative thoughts and emotions, because in her they can't exist. Ask Mother Mary to take those negative feelings from you before you hurt someone. If you don't feel like you have a connection to Mother Mary, go on your knees in private immediately and pray for three people for five minutes and those negatives feelings, whatever they are, will vanish. You will not be bothered by them anymore because you actively made a decision that you did not want to feel bad or negative.

When you dislike a situation, change it. Have the intestinal fortitude to make things happen in your life that you want to happen. That is using the masculine energy. Do not allow anything to take you off your center of balance or your inner peace. If you let things disturb your peace, you are choosing those things. If you let disturbances into your psyche, then you are not being protective of your temple, the place where only God should be. You are admitting things into your atmosphere and body, mind and emotions that God does not bless. You are indulging parts of yourself that are soiling the very nature of your temple because you are permitting energies into your vibratory space that are so different from the energy of God who made you.

"You must believe," He says, "that man should worry only about making himself rich in virtue. But mind you: you must not worry anxiously or painfully. Good is the enemy of anxiety, of fears, of haste, which still show too many traces of avarice, jealousy and human mistrust. Let your work be constant, confident, peaceful, without rough starts and stops....Be peaceful in victory and peaceful in defeat. Also tears shed for an error you made and which grieves you because by it you have displeased God, must be peaceful, comforted by humility and trust. [Frustration], anger against oneself are always a symptom of pride and lack of confidence. He who is humble knows that he is a poor man subject to the miseries of the flesh, which at times triumphs. He who is humble puts his trust not so much in himself as in God, and is serene also when defeated and says: "Forgive me, Father, I know that You are aware of my weakness which overwhelms me at times. I will believe that You pity me. I am fully confident that You will help me in the future even more than heretofore, notwithstanding I please You so little." Do not be indifferent or avaricious with regard to the gifts of God. Give generously what you possess of wisdom and virtue" (*The Poem of the Man-God*, Vol. 3, p. 11-12).

"The Kingdom of The King of kings will come. But not according to human standards. Not with regard to what perishes; but with regard to what is eternal. You do not enter it along a flowery road of triumph or on a carpet made purple by enemy blood; but climbing a steep path of sacrifices and a mild staircase of forgiveness and love. Our victories over ourselves will give us that Kingdom" (*The Poem of the Man-God*, Vol. 3, p. 325).

"But to suffer is not to sin. It is expiation. And as a repentant drunkard commits no sin but gains merits if he resists the stimulus heroically and does not drink anymore, so he who has sinned, and repents and resists all stimuli, gains merit and will not lack supernatural help to resist. It is not a sin to be tempted. On the contrary it is a battle that brings victory. And believe me, in God there is only the desire to forgive and help who has done wrong but has later repented..." (*The Poem of the Man-God*, Vol. 3, p. 350-351).

"'There is peace for men of good will.' Peace! That is, success, victory on the Earth and in Heaven, because God is with those who are willing to obey Him. God does not look so much at the high-sounding deeds that man does on his own initiative, as at the humble, prompt, faithful obedience to the work which He proposes" (*The Poem of the Man-God*, Vol. 3, p. 706).

"God will be with you if you are humble, if you admit that by yourselves you can do nothing, whereas you can do everything if you are united to the Father.... In fact men busy themselves in vain, if God does not assist their efforts. Whereas he wins without bustling about, who trusts in the Lord, Who knows when it is right to reward people with victories, and when it is just to punish with defeats. Foolish is the person who wants to judge God, advising or criticizing Him. Can you imagine an ant, which watching the work of a marble-cutter, should say: 'You are no good at doing that. I could do better and quicker than you.' He who wants to teach God, cuts the same poor figure. And to his ridiculous figure he adds ingratitude and arrogance, forgetting what he is: a creature, and what God is: the Creator. Now if God created such a perfect creature, who may think that they can advise God Himself, what will be the perfection of the Author of all creatures, be like? That simple thought should be enough to abase pride, destroying that wicked satanic plant, the parasite which creeps into man's intellect and destroys it, and supplants, suffocates and kills every good tree, every virtue which makes man great on the Earth, really great, not because of great wealth or crowns, but because of justice and supernatural wisdom, and makes him happy in Heaven for ever and ever" (*The Poem of the Man-God*, Vol. 3, p. 757).

Chapter Two

The Law of Karma: Giving and Receiving

Everybody knows what the law of karma is but some people are a little confused. Karma means that if you put out bad things then bad things will probably happen, and if you put out good things then good things will happen. It's inexorable. Jesus said it a different way: "As you sow so shall you reap." What you think puts out energy that goes out and does some things and comes back to you. It is an ancient teaching. What it defies is the mythology in our world that accidents happen; or bad things happen to good people; or God does things to people. God does not force anybody and God does not interfere with your choices. Yes, you have two things that you're not in control of: you're not in control of your birth and you're not in control of your death. Birth and death are the domain of God. So if you take control over your death by force you have a huge debt to pay because it is not your department. It is none of your business. Your job is to figure out how you are going to live, and the quality of your life and what you are going to put out. What you create in your mind and what you create in your feelings is what determines what comes back to you. That is not a popular subject. People like the word karma because they don't know what it means. Something about our country seems fascinated with the East, because we always like those Eastern words when we don't know what they mean.

How many of you think that it is really a shame that God lets bad things happen to people? How many of you secretly find that a useful thought to explain away your responsibility? When something unpleasant happens, do you know that you needed to experience it? Do you know why you needed to experience it? Or did you create a hitch in your prayer and in how you were thinking that allowed something funny to come to your life? The unpopular part of a real spiritual path is that you are completely responsible for what you create and you are completely responsible for your present moment, which also determines your future. You are responsible for what happened. You may not know how you created it, or you may not have been able to tell that a certain kind of thinking is going to produce a particular result, or that desires you are indulging are going to produce a particular kind of hell. You may not know that yet, but if you pay more attention you will see it.

When you are dense, slow, and sluggish, and when the life force does not move very fast in you, things do not change very often in you. Things are drawn out, tedious and take a lot of time, because the law of cause and effect works very slowly for you. It works in proportion with how much power is moving in your thought and how much power is moving in your body, in your will and in your wanting. If not much power is moving in you, we would wonder if that is convenient for you, to not have much power. When you do not have much power and energy moving in you, you can get other people to take responsibility for you. You can have other people help you because you cannot get it done, or it takes so long, or it is too hard, so you actually enlist other people. There is karma for that because you make other people pay for your not being able to do it. You make other people responsible when you could have done it and you didn't do it. There is karma in ripping other people off for the thing that you should have taken care of.

How long does the law of cause and effect, the law of karma, take to come back around to you? Imagine that you are on the highway and having a fit with somebody in the next car. Most of you have certain opinions about what other people do in their cars. For instance, say you get angry at somebody beside you, and you are intellectually educating them in your mind, and you put out a certain poisonous toxic fume, and you say some really bad things and hammer on the wheel, and you are yelling or growling. Some vocalizations, expletives and things that only you would know and hear come out of your mouth. When the traffic clears up you are fine. You feel much better and the sun is shining and everything is bright again and you forget that you did that. You forget because you do not want to feel accountable and you rarely ever fix anything that you put out.

It might take two or three months for that negative thought that you hammered on that driver to come back around to you. It goes whoosh, whoosh, like a boomerang; you get hit on the side of the head three months later and you say, "God, why does this have to happen to me?' And you have no memory that you put that crap out. And there it is back in your face. Then you say, "God is so random." And you put all the responsibility on someone else. You put it out and you got it back and you just did not see how long it took and you did not see what the cause was, because you are oblivious and do not do daily retrospections and examine yourself at the end of the day. You would have seen that you got really mad at some driver and said some pretty mean things and never asked to be forgiven or apologized to them or to God, and never asked that God would not let that boomerang keep going. You did not say, "Please stop that, I didn't mean it." Because that will stop it. And then you make a prayer to bless that person that you just cursed. You do not think it is a curse, but you cursed them. Yeah, it is subtle. And you wonder why that law of karma comes back to you. Why? So you will know what you put out.

Most people put out plenty of negative energy. I call it the P word or the E word depending on whether you prefer pride or entitlement. Really, are you so good that you are entitled to special treatment? "Whatever I put out shouldn't come back to me." Are you so special that you deserve exemptions from the law of karma? There is punishment at the judgment that is very similar to karma. After you leave your body, you get to see what you put out during your life. You go through a three day retrospection of your life where it is viewed by you with powers bigger than you. It is a loving experience but it is the facts, not any subjective shaming going on. It is seeing what you did and didn't give, and what you could have learned and failed to learn or accomplish. You see what you came into a body to learn and didn't do. All of that is going to come right up in your face at the end of life and be a little judgment for you. You will experience the karma of having to come back and redo the things you did not do, or take care of the things you did not take care of, or come back and learn the things you failed or refused to learn. Now, you could call that punishment. I don't. I call it justice. Like a kid who does half-assed mediocre work in 2nd grade and the principal decides that this particular student has to do 2nd grade again. You might call that a punishment. I call that a supportive response, supporting that kid in making sure they understand 2nd grade work well enough for them to feel confident in it to move on. It is all justice and it is all clear. It says you do not know the material, so you must learn it again. That is how we are treated in God.

What comes back karmically has your name on it, like special delivery, FedEx, just for you. It is very precise and very realistic; it is very perfect. You should thank God for such a network of perfection. Once I got a really fun parking ticket in Oakland. I had parked under a tree where the branches obscured a sign that I was not able to see, apparently. It said something like, "Every other day, don't park here." Something like that. They say it in language some people can understand. But I did not see it or read it and I parked there on a Wednesday and I should have been parking there on Tuesday and I am sorry about that and I got a $43 ticket. And I am thinking, "God, OK, that's a very expensive lunch, lunch with tip for $43, I mean that's a good tip." But that's not what I really thought. I thought, "I bet I really owe somebody $43 that I failed to pay a long time ago. I probably got something for $43 cheaper than it should have been and this caught me up to the actual fee that I should have paid." And then I thought, "OK, if I can't remember anything specifically that I owe to someone, I can probably scan a few other lives where I might have taken some stuff from people, or I might have taken advantage of some people, or I might have stolen some stuff, shorted somebody on something, or been mean to somebody and it was $43 of meanness and I needed to pay that back." So in lots of ways it was perfect because God gave me the gift of having that paid. Now most of you do not react well to these things. Not only that, you usually send out another boomerang. Am I right? Now you have that coming to you because of your prideful self-righteousness that you do not deserve these kinds of horrible things happening to little innocent you, when in fact you totally deserved that and it was totally just. In fact that would have evened the score, but you then made it worse by your attitude. Attitude is everything in my world. That is why being around a teacher is so disturbing. Their perspective is so different.

Attitude puts out energy into the mind, and you can certainly feel hostility in another car if someone is putting that out towards you. Not in the way they drive necessarily, although the sound of the horn might give it away. But subtly you can feel anger from the person behind or next to you. When people put out energy you can feel it. For example, when you go into somebody's home you can feel the energy of the house. You can feel whether the house is kind of slow-minded or whether it is stuffy or congested or whether it is heavy or really sad or stuck or nasty, dark, mean energy. You can feel all that. The paint, walls, windows, floors, rugs and furniture soak up the energy of the people living in that house. The whole area is oozing with their energy. There are people who like to be mad, and if they are already mad then they get mean – sometimes they even wear clerical garb on Sundays. Some of them say heavy-handed things to people to try to make them feel bad, thinking that will motivate them into goodness. I have not seen people motivated into being good by scaring them half to death. It has been tried for 2,000 years and has not worked.

Karma means you are completely responsible for creating what is happening to you right now. It is not random; you just lost consciousness of what you put out and failed to remember it. If you have an attitude thing, it is going to go out into the mass mind; it is going to cause a vibration. That vibration is going to attract other people who have those kinds of attitudes. That is how wars are created, by a bunch of people who hate something. If you hate anything, if you hate an idea, if you hate a food, if you hate a part of your body, you are contributing to war. Some of you are body part haters, and have selected parts of your body that you are at war with. You enjoy the freedom of attacking a certain part of your body that God created, and you hate it. All those little hatreds of relatives and friends, arguments and squabbles and hardness of hearts that you have, they all go out and accumulate over a city. Then those energies float in the atmosphere and move around the earth to a volatile area where there are warlords struggling, and then a war breaks out because we all contributed to it. That is our karma. Every war that happens, we have all participated in – unless you have been peaceful since the last war. If you have been completely peaceful in your heart, never had an attitude problem, never had any anger, and never had a fiercely aggressive emotion that was hostile to anyone else, then you can say you never participated in war. But not one of you can say that. As a result, every one of us is responsible for every single war on this planet. You think it is just the two factions fighting?

They were just the volatile places that you contributed to. If you want to take responsibility, that is responsibility.

There is city karma, political karma, country karma, and there is a great deal of family karma. A whole family might have decided to shut down their hearts over five or six generations, and this created weak hearts manifesting in a genetic visible proof that their hearts are damaged. They rationalize it by saying the whole family has a genetic propensity. They shut down their hearts and stopped loving in very subtle ways. Now it affects the genes of everyone born in that family line. They could fix that, but it would take a lot of work because there is a whole train behind them. It is the same with diabetes or any other long-term development of emotionally created illnesses. They were created in the family, and the family buys into it, and people born into that family accept it or think they need it and that is what they get. These patterns do not show up for four or five generations and then gradually the chromosomes show the genetic changes. The human body can take a lot of abuse and will not get unhealthy for a while. Younger people can trash their bodies and put out all kinds of angry stuff and do a lot of alcohol and drugs and apparently nothing happens to them. Then, later in life the effects start to show up. It has to symptomatize in the body if you have been putting it out. It has to, unless you have healed it. The genetics are not that important. The transformational, healing work we do is not only good for the earth, it is also intimately good for those people who are ill. But do not get fooled into attending to the body too much because you are going to leave this world and this body. If you change your body into light and heal it and make it come alive, you will have mastered that part of yourself. When you leave this body you will be in better shape next time.

Stupid, crazy things that people do to each other reap tremendous karma. Nobody is completely innocent ever, because we cannot see the whole picture. The powerful ones takes precedence and then push the weaker ones around and there is some more karma. The United States has huge karma. We are hated by many countries for our interference in many, many governments. We have overthrown regimes and almost always install the wrong person in leadership and then train them in our military, and then they turn against us, and we fight with them and it kind of goes on and on. We never learn our lessons. We train them in our military technology, we give them all our weapon systems, and then they use those against us. That is how it works and it has been happening for 70 years. We will do it again until people get sick of it. And people are not sick of war. Now we, who are sleeping, let our leaders do whatever they want to do. We are responsible. Our karma is that we did not say anything about these things and we did not care and we did not vote against it.

We are expert at pouting, acting out, having a myriad of ego and attitude problems on this planet. This is because we all are attracted here by our similar level of development: juvenile delinquents, basically stubborn, hard-headed people. For example, if I tell someone to stop having fits, they will go right out and teach me a lesson by having one that afternoon, since most people cannot stand to have anyone telling them what to do. Alright, these are the kind of people I like to work with. It hearkens back to my history of having been one of these. That is how I understand them. That must be why I like to work with them.

When most people say, "That's your karma," it usually means someone is suffering something. If you are philosophical about it, that is one thing. However, if you are gleeful that karma is going to come around to somebody, then you are being mean or angry. You are gloating on the fact that their demise is coming. You have a vindictive charge in you that likes to gloat when others suffer. That is meanness. God is wise and wants us to learn that when we put things out we are going to get them back. That makes sense. You should be sad when people get what is coming back to them. It is sad they put those things out, and it is cosmically just when they come back to them. It is because of our density that we have to go through such pain in order to learn.

It is justice and yet the instruments through which the karma is delivered also have to pay. For example, let us look at child abuse. Those who suffered from that as children may have needed the experience in order to feel what it is like on the helpless end of things. As a child, you are helpless and not in control of the family. You are a victim of whatever the parents are going to put out. Ultimately, you need the experience of what that feels like. That means you were the abuser before. I am not blaming, I am just showing the justice of it over lifetimes. However, the parents who treat children badly have new karma, and if they were mean or careless or did not pay attention to you, or were addicted or whatever, they have new karma to work out and pay for. When you emancipate from your parents, you can be free of that. It is unusual to be born into a conscious family with spiritually developed parents. It is quite rare. There is a long waiting list for them. Most people do not want to wait ten years to incarnate because there is an urgency to incarnate now so they just choose between three or four parental options.

We could avoid a lot of negative karma by learning to be clear and honest in our relationships. Most people rarely honestly ever go to somebody and say, "I thought really bad thoughts about you today and I'm really sorry." You say to yourself, "What they don't know won't hurt them." Wrong. You did hurt them even if they never know. Why not be honest and go tell them. OK, you see the level of accountability that we are not used to. You put negative energy out and it went somewhere and you went to work. Everything is fine and you are in a good mood, happy as a clam at high tide. It may take a while for the karma to return, because you are not very powerful in your thinking and have not learned to use power. You have not learned to be a lighted being that has a lot of energy moving inside you, or how to have things move when you want them to, or how to get your prayers moving really quickly. Most of your thoughts go out really slowly into the mind of God, like a boomerang, and goes whoosh, whoosh, whoosh. You need to understand that everything that goes around comes around and what you put out it comes back to you.

If someone says something hurtful to you, your job is to find out what they really mean. What if they are really mad and trying to hurt you? Then ask them, "Were you trying to hurt me?" They might answer, "Yes, I was so mad at you." You can respond, "Oh, I wasn't sure, I kind of felt some of that. Do you still feel that way?" And they might say, "yes." What should you do when you make a mistake, in a typically polite society (which we do not always have)? You would apologize. And that would fix it, wouldn't it? If you apologized to me, I would forgive you because that is my job. I would love to, I am kind of anxious to, I would like to do it now, can you help me forgive you? When you say "I'm sorry" and you mean it, I feel great! And we are done. I do forgive you, thanks. We are done, we can clear that up now. That is the best way to do it. What if the person says, "No, I did not have anything negative going on at all." Then you apologize, saying, "I'm sorry because I was about ready to jump on you and that is my fault. I was ready to react and I should not have. I should have asked you first, but I was geared up to hurt you." Be honest and apologize because you made a judgment that you did not check out beforehand. You did not wait to ask and were ready to pounce on them. That is mean and you need to apologize. These are very simple things. You need to communicate. If you do not communicate, you are hiding. And it is probably because of pride. In a spiritual community, that stuff should be open. That is so quickly fixable. Nobody will hold it against you because that would not be loving and we recommend loving people. See what I mean? Am I being simple enough?

That kind of honesty and realness is not established yet in the world. In full positive thinking, maybe you could be able to do that. Maybe you could infiltrate some of your places of work with a little bit of realness or possibly an actual real conversation every now and then just to startle them into something. We would want all the human beings to be able to communicate like this. Real, clear straight, no B.S. This creates a condition where everything is resolvable, it is easy, and everybody cops to their stuff, and nobody is too prideful to say I am sorry. And nobody is afraid to admit that they went weird on you. Because that is a lack of honesty. It is pride, ego and self-protection. God does not need protection. Why do you protect your ego? Your ego is garbage. Mine is, too. I do not have a special mantle place for my ego. It would make me gag walking in looking at that. God should be up there, not me.

Being as dense as we are, we do not always know what we are putting out, so we have to get a very slow lesson; we put it out and eventually it comes back. When you stop putting that kind of garbage out, you will not have that kind of thing coming back any more. So how long does it take for all the clean up? Let us say you put out only good things for three months. I would say you are almost getting to the place where those bad things will not come back. Maybe it will take three to nine months, depending on how negative and brutal you have been. It depends on how willful and stubborn you have been, how long it takes for that karma to clear up. How do you clear it up? Do not put out negative energy anymore and things will clear up. Put out good things, blessings and prayers and happy thoughts for people, positive that will speed the process up. The most powerful thing to clear up karma is to give it away, give it back to God, give your stuff to God. We do that through communion, we do that through blessings and here is the thing that no other path has, no other path on the earth has, except the Christian path and that is forgiveness. You have forgiveness, grace and mercy that are given by the teachers of this path, Jesus and Mary. They give you forgiveness and they wipe it away, just for the asking. There is no other path that does that. Forgiveness, blessings, mercy and good behavior can clear negative karma. The solution is in your own environment, which is your body. Are fear, anger, pride, egotism, selfishness, retaliation, aggression, and reactivity in you? Those are the things that are going to pollute our world. They have polluted the world since humans have been on the planet. Can other people still get a rise out of you? Then you do not have control over yourself. You still have buttons that make you go ballistic if people push them, which means you do not have control over yourself. You have not said, "no way will I act like that again." Do you know why you do not say that? Because you want the option to freak out. Try this if you want to understand the inner reality of environmentalism. Get really angry by putting a really bad poison into your blood and then spread it all around through your whole body. Was that graphic enough for you? Everything you put out spreads through your whole body. You get it first before anyone else gets it. You have got to get a grip on yourself if you want to feel better. You will feel better when you create a better environment in your feeling and thinking, and your body will respond with peace. Your body is completely responsive to you.

Forgiveness is not saying, "I know my parents did the best they could" or "They did really badly, but I let that go," and then you watch for the same problem in everyone else. You have not forgiven them for it yet, if you are watching for it everywhere. Until we find a teacher that can teach us those skills, we are kind of at a loss. There is an assumption that people make, that you were not protected as a child, and that you had to do all the protecting yourself. The fact is you were totally protected from it being a whole lot worse. There was grace there, or you could have been killed or much more abused or neglected. You could have been starved or abandoned on the street corner of some town. A thousand bad things could have happened that did not happen because of one thing, the good karma from the past and God's love for you. The real defender of you as a human being is God, and you have been protected from thousands of things. The prideful presumption that all this protection was accomplished by your resources is ridiculous. Your life is preserved and continues by God's breath in you and God's attention on you. You would not exist if God dropped His attention from you, and yet you think you are the one running the show. That is totally ridiculous. You would have no consciousness, no intelligence, no will, no power, and no ability to love or receive love if God was not in you. It is all pride. You build this huge castle on the fact that if you were not vigilant, you would not exist. You can relax because protection is not your department. Your life was a gift, and it always is and you do not own it.

The only thing that is happening to us is what was deserve. Karma: what you put out you are getting back. Then you complain that it is too much for you. No, it is not too much for you. It was not too much when you put it out. You are totally responsible for what happens to you and you could be very conscious of what you put out. You have just what you created. Now maybe you will create something good. Why do we not change our attitude and start trusting now? I do not have to defend myself, because if God wants to hurt me, fine. Why? How can I say that? Because I feel God's love in or out of a body. This body is nothing. I take care of it but it is nothing. It will go away. And I will still be loved. What I do is what God wants me to do. So I do not care about anyone else's opinion. The real part of me is God. God does not need any defense. The more one with God I become, the less I need to have any protection or any defense whatsoever. You have no reason to protect yourself. You might have felt unsafe as a child, which karmically you might have needed. But you are not a child anymore and you are not in your family, so you do not have to take that abuse from them anymore. Now you get to choose. You are completely safe, and if something does happen to you, check to see if you were being foolish. Did you put yourself in harm's way? Let it be a learning experience. You do not see the half of it. God does.

Chapter Three

Transformation: Creating the Life You Want

What is it that transforms you? You might say that grace is what transforms you. But I want to focus on what causes us to change. What is it that motivates a disciple to change? What would you tell someone who is hoping that their life changes and transforms for the better?

First of all, we need a person who wants to change. We need a person who wants to let go of certain faults or problems, a person who feels the need to have some things removed or modified in their personality in order to start the process. If we want to change, we have to notice that something is not working as well as we want it to. We need to have a feeling about what it is that we are noticing about ourselves, like if you see a troubling character trait in yourself like worrying or a bad temper. If you do not see this trait, you cannot change it. If you see it or if others start pointing it out to you, you take notice and begin to ask yourself what it is doing there in you. If you have feelings about it, then you are taking the first step towards transformation. Your feelings motivate some decision. There are quite a few more steps to finally getting that trait transformed.

To break it down, we need someone who wants change. We need to notice something that needs changing. We definitely should be aware of why we are keeping things the way they are. What do we get out of it? We need to understand a little of what is making it persist inside us. We need to be tired of it or downright disgusted. Then we need to want it transformed and removed from us. We do not want it inside of us anymore. This is a critical part of the transformative process that we sometimes overlook or ignore. At this point, we are unable on our own power to do anything about it because we need help. So we ask for help from God, Jesus, Mary, and our teachers to help remove this pattern. We need to participate with them by seeing the opposite of the pattern and feeling what it would be like if the positive, opposite pattern were acting instead of the negative one. Finally, we will have to act the new pattern out, stepping out on our prayer and wish that the new be installed and the old discarded.

The action of transformation occurs when something larger than you and your small understanding helps you with what you want. In fact, the universal law operates for anyone who activates it with will or desire – in other words, with wanting or feeling. Your willingness is your decision to have it removed or changed, while your wanting is your strong feeling that you have about a change. If you really want something, you can have it. If you really feel strongly about something, the universal law will be activated and the God force will bring it to you. This is the way the universal law works for all of creation. So if something is not the way you want it to be, then change it to what you do want. It is possible for everyone and it works perfectly for all. Jesus said, "It is God's good pleasure to give you the Kingdom" and "God satisfies the desire of every living thing."

In the Tree of Life lessons, it says that our use of the one mind activates the spirit of God to provide what we want. Your will, decision, want and desire activate the spirit of God to provide, through the universal law inherent in God's being, everything you have decided. It is that simple. I often say that it is all about wanting. If you would just decide what you want, then you can have it all.

What if you have things you would like to change within yourself? Why do you have to have a battle with yourself whenever you need to change something? Why do you have to resist so much, when it would be so easy to just create it in mind and let the transformative power of God's grace take care of it for you? The priests in our order have had the experience quite often of just holding something in mind and within a few hours or days what they had in mind manifests in their waking reality. It is taken care of as simply and certainly as what you ate for breakfast this morning. If the power of God does not manifest in your material reality, then you have cut off God's power from connecting to you and from loving you. God moves in creation, so why do you not let God move inside of you and take care of the things you need and want? Nothing is impossible for those who love God, as Jesus stated in the New Testament.

So, what can go wrong? Well, there are many things that you can do to trip yourself up so that you will not get something you want. What if a substantial part of you wants to change but a little part of you does not want things to change? Then you are struggling inside, holding on to the way things have been while another part of you wants to move on and grow. I would suggest that you have all those parties come to the table, have a meeting and air out all of the wants and wishes, all the fears and concerns, to see what the trouble is. This is where a spiritual teacher can really help you get these parts expressing with a clear voice. I cannot imagine it would be very hard for you to understand yourself if you listen to every part that has a say on the matter. Then you can make a considered decision. Once those parts that fear or resist change can be heard, they will lose their intensity, fear and pride and you can relax into deciding what is best. I know you may have intense resistance to change because of how hurt you have been in the past and how you imagine that your present life is just like it was then. But that was then, and this is now. The situation you find yourself in today is totally different than before and the people who had power then have no power over you now. If you pray to see how things really are, you will see that you are in a wholly different condition.

When you say you want to change some things and a recurring pattern of not being able to change occurs, there is a simple explanation. You do not really want to. If you want to stand up out of your seat, you will because you can. Nothing can stop you when you really want to stand up. When you really want to get rid of something in your house, you throw it out, do not you? You do not worry about it or fret over it. It is the same with any character trait or problem. There is nothing stopping you and no one preventing you from doing whatever you want, or expressing whatever quality you want. It is up to you. In psychotherapy when a person says "I can't," we have them say, "I won't." This makes it very clear that they have to take responsibility for preventing themselves from growing and moving on. When people are stuck on something inside themselves and claims to be failing at making things change, the teachers are instructed to let you sit in your soup until you are good and sick of it. When you want to move on, you will. But your teacher will not force you to change anything. You have to want to and volunteer for it. We know what to do if you want our help.

Now I want to talk about the part of the transformation process that you cannot do yourself. You need help and you cannot do these things alone. You cannot do anything without God's energy. This teaches you that you cannot make good changes without the power of God. God can enter only by invitation because God wants you to voluntarily ask for help and allow God to enter into your life and process. When God enters, grace enters because all of a sudden a whole new energy and power is applied to whatever you are focusing on. God's grace moves where there is humility and a sincere wish for help. God's grace also moves where effort has been applied in the direction of your wants and wishes. In other words, you can turn a car wheel easier if the car is rolling than when it is standing still. God can help you better if you begin to move in the direction of what you want. This means if you are already acting in the direction of what you are looking to express, then grace will come in and give you a big nudge in the direction of your wish. Grace cannot move where there is no receptivity to God. God wants you to be happy. God wants you to be free. There is nothing in you that cannot be changed unless you have made a karmic decision before you came in to this life to live with a certain condition.

There seems to be a mass mind conception on the earth of what it takes to make a change in yourself. People seem to think that is nearly impossible, that it is extraordinarily difficult to change emotions, family patterns, bodily aches and pains and just about everything else. Everything important is seen as difficult under this lens. Your limitations are not the way God thinks or feels. Limitations are not the way of grace and not the way of God. When you get on your knees in prayer and truly ask God sincerely for help, God will come flying to you to help. But even though you figured it was prudent to ask God and to admit that you have something that needs change and help, will you let God help you? I have seen many people ask for help and then turn right around and block that help every time. They are afraid to let go and let God just because they might lose some nostalgic sentiment from the past. But then they do not really want any changes rocking their world. They want things to stay the way they are, or they want things to go back the way they were. They are living in the past with the old voices constantly nagging in their heads. Very little can be expected from such a person as they are not malleable to God and not humble before their Creator. No grace can move in such a one because they are blocking God by not letting go. They are doing everything themselves and making sure nothing disturbs the sleep of their world. It is very sad in that case.

But if a person gets on their knees and opens their mind and heart, and lets go of everything they are holding onto and gives it all up, then God comes running and pours graces into their soul, mind, heart and body. As much as they are able to receive at that moment comes flooding into them and the love of God, moving in grace, takes care of them and lifts them up on angel's wings.

"…you are dearer to Me than if you were my own children, because you are children of My spirit. I have led your spirits to the Life and I will do so even more. Bear in mind, in memory of Me, bear in mind that I bless you for the thoughts you had in your hearts. But grow in justice, by wanting only what gives honor to the true God for whom you must have absolute love, such as is given to no other creature. Come to this perfect justice that I am setting as an example to you, the justice that tramples on the selfishness of one's own welfare, on the fear of enemies and of death, on everything, to do the will of God. Prepare your spirits. The dawn of Grace is rising. The banquet of Grace is being prepared. Your souls, the souls of those who want to come to the Truth, are at the eve of their wedding, of their liberation, of their redemption. Prepare yourselves in justice for the feast of Justice" (*The Poem of the Man-God*, Vol. 5, p. 258).

"If the world did not see the redness of My Wounds, it would really soon forget that a God sacrificed Himself for its sins, it would forget that I really died in the most cruel torture, it would forget which is the balm for its wounds. Here is the balm. Come and kiss it. Each kiss is an increase of purification and grace for you. I solemnly tell you that purification and grace are never sufficient, because the world consumes what is infused by Heaven and it is necessary to counterbalance the ruins of the world by means of Heaven and its treasures. I am Heaven. All Heaven is in Me, and the celestial treasures flow from the open wounds." He stretches out His hands to be kissed by His Apostles. And He has to press His wounded Hands against the eager timid lips, because the fear of increasing His pain prevents those lips from pressing against those wounds" (*The Poem of the Man-God*, Vol. 5, p. 764).

"So I washed you before admitting you to the Eucharistic banquet, before listening to the confession of your sins, before infusing the Holy Spirit into you and consequently the character of both true Christians reconfirmed in Grace, and of My Priests. Let the same be done to the others whom you will have to prepare for the Christian life.

Baptize with water in the Name of the God One and Trine and in My Name and through My infinite merits, so that the Original Sin may be cancelled from hearts, sins may be remitted, Grace and the Holy Virtues may be infused, and the Holy Spirit may descend to dwell in consecrated temples, that is, in the bodies of people living in the Grace of the Lord" (*The Poem of the Man-God*, Vol. 5, p. 842-843).

Make every effort to open to God's grace. Allow God to work on you to perfect you and build within you such openness to be led and guided, such sensitivity to every inspiration from God, so much infusion of love from God who loved you enough to create you with such freedom and beauty. Let God perfect you according to God's design and you will be at peace and flooded with life and grace.

Chapter Four

Choosing the Spiritual Path

If you track the thread of spiritual inclinations in your life, you will find that certain themes repeated themselves to you over the course of years. Trace back to the first time you felt some longing for God, some feeling for the purpose of life. When was that? Where were you on the planet at that time? Were you really young or was it later? How do you know that you were not just around when someone just happened to be talking about it and it seemed like an interesting thing to pursue? Did you really have a choice or did you put out a strong prayer before you came into this life to follow God and do God's work here on the planet?

If you are honest and think about it a little, you will find that your heart longed for and hoped for God at some point in your life. Maybe you had to see the difference between your parents' love and consistency and what your soul remembers of God's love and consistency. Many people have made strong prayers to be awakened in this life as soon as possible so that they can be about God's business. If you are one of the ones who found the path by accident and were not expecting to have a life in any way relating to serving God, then you have to do some special examination of whether you were really called or just wandered into the spiritual path on one of the explorations of your journey. This may sound strange to you, but there are a lot of different reasons for wanting spiritual development or spiritual training. Sometimes a friend of yours is moving into the spiritual life and you do not want to lose connection with them. Sometimes you feel that it would be interesting and your life is boring, so why not pursue and learn about the spiritual path for a while, especially while nothing major is happening in your life. If the reason you are on the spiritual path is for any other reason than to serve God because you love Jesus Christ and you love God, then you are going to run into problems as you grow because you are responsible for the things you learn and for what you hear. When you receive a truth or a teaching that is real, you are responsible to apply that teaching in your life and let it change things. This truth will transform your life if you practice it and put some consistent attention into it.

If you have been changing and growing for some time and you are moving right along, at some point you will be called to give up something or change something that is not so easy. When this happens, the ego smarts a little and screams at you that you were not informed that anything major had to change. You get upset that something so important or earth shaking is being called into question. You get a little angry that the teacher suggests that you submit the issue to God for guidance and let God guide you. You are startled that you are being asked to let God enter into an area that you yourself had roped off as sacred and off limits. You made a previous decision relating to this area stating that it was fine the way it is and no changes would be permitted. It is just about at this time that the teacher points out that holding the old pattern is blocking your spiritual progress and getting in the way of what you are growing into. Your ego yells back, "I was never sure I really wanted this path anyway." Then all hell breaks loose as you fight and struggle with whether you are going to go on and grow or just cut your losses and do something else. Every student on the spiritual path goes through a crisis of decision like this at some point on the path. No one is exempt from it. When it happens depends on the person and how serious the fenced off area is inside you.

Of course, we warn everyone clearly at the beginning of training that their life will not be their own and you may not recognize yourself if you change very much. You are being asked by Jesus and Mary to give over everything you have, all your possessions. These possessions are not so much material things, as those are the easiest to give up. You are being asked to stop thinking the way you have and to give up preserving parts of yourself that you decided others would hurt if you didn't protect them. You are being asked to trust the masters, Jesus and Mary, even when you are not sure you can or you should. But then, you are informed that if you do not make the attempt to trust, you will never be sure if you can. You cannot know the masters unless you turn your life over to them. You cannot turn your life over to them unless you have enough faith to begin trusting them.

It is so painful to watch you struggle for each inch of giving over to God. You seem so tortured being on the spiritual path that I often want to relieve you of what appears to be so burdensome and troublesome. Out of compassion for you I want you to be happy, and if you think that doing your own thing and not serving God is going to make you happy, then I want you to pursue that. When you find out what a mirage in the desert your desires really are, you might be humble enough and grateful enough to Jesus Christ and Mother Mary to give your life over to them and serve them. I do not want to torture you. But I am totally bewildered that you think you could find anything interesting in the world that would compare to the God Self and God's love for you. What God has for each of you is the realization of who you really are, which is God. God has total communion waiting for each of you, total ecstasy and bliss. God has complete love for you and close personal connection because God knows you completely. Everything about you is completely transparent to God and you cannot hide anything from God or the masters, Jesus and Mary. Your teachers are also very much aware of your whole predicament and all of your challenges.

When the tables turn and you finally get how much you are loved, you are awed and amazed. You are sad for all of the trouble you have been to God and your teachers. You are embarrassed by your silly little fears and doubts. You are humbled to the point of not caring what other people think anymore because you have God loving you and speaking to you in a deep relationship inside you. Then you are converted. You are changed into a true disciple of Jesus and Mary. You know you have gone through a rite of passage because you no longer waffle or waver on the path. At this point, nothing can sway you or tempt you from devoting your whole life to God. You are God's and you know that you are completely devoted to God's work on the earth. You would no more be able to think of doing anything else than you would think of going into the darkness. Everything becomes fulfilling and joyful because you have finally put God first and you know it. You are sure of it and nothing is going to get in your way of serving and expressing what God wants for you. That is a joy to behold for the teachers because then we can count on you completely and we know you are solid. We know you are becoming fully one with Jesus and Mary and your transformations and growth becomes exponential from then on. You think that people just grow until they are ordained as deacons or priests? Watch what happens to them a year or three after taking on those ordinations. They are transformed from their former lives and are almost unrecognizable from the disaster they were when they started on the path.

Disaster or train wreck might actually describe how you are before you begin real spiritual training. You may not know who you are or why you are on the planet. You probably still define yourself by what your head knows or what your ego keeps telling you. You may think in terms of separations and differences rather than seeing everything and everyone as an expression of God. Perhaps you are fearful, worry a lot, compare yourself with others and compete with those who you feel are getting more love than you are. All of this is through your limited sight and limited understanding of how things work. Our teachers are patient with reckless opinions and misuse of analytical or critical abilities. They will love you through your holding on and letting go, knowing that the God within you is emerging gradually and surely. The teacher holds your eventual emancipation in mind and sacrifices everything so that you might know God first hand. The priest or teacher will continue to represent the truth and the reality until you have the experience of it yourself. If they held onto the picture you have of yourself before you began training, they would be praying for you to stay the way you were. That is negative prayer. They see your perfection and divinity and empower that with all of their love, patience, understanding and knowing. Their prayer for you is that you become one with God, free from the wheel of karma and completely converted to the mission that Jesus and Mary are calling us to do. There is nothing else.

In Maria Valtorta's *The Notebooks 1943*, Jesus says:

"I understand and sympathize with your sadness. It is not that sadness which I denounce as a sin.

Blameworthy sadness is that which comes from un-willingness to accept things and crosses – the former being human – and the latter, supernatural. Blamewor-thy sadness is the thirst for enjoyment, wealth, a thirst which is not satisfied and which brings you sadness, or a thirst which, after being sated, leaves you sadder than before, because conscience weeps in you. This is the sadness which I condemn.

But the good sadness, felt more over the misfortunes of others than over one's own, the grief caused by seeing God offended, the affliction over bonds of love which are broken – I do not condemn that. I experienced it before you and I wept.
Moreover, when a soul rises even higher and not only possesses in herself a sadness which is not condem-nable, but is able to give Me that sadness of hers so that I may use her tears for the good of others, then I take this soul and cradle her over my Heart to lull her affliction to sleep and give her my joy.

You feel it. I know that you feel it seeping into you.

Those jolts of relief you feel, which seem to you sunbeams in the darkness coming to you from many things, and which seem to you liberation from the burdens prostrating you, are Me coming into you with my joy.

You also have intuited the origin of so much darkness in the pain invading you for your good. Yes. You, by living in Me and for Me, unleash the wrath of the Enemy, and he, unable to do anything else, seeks to terrify you by rendering the future blacker than it already is. But do not be afraid. I am with you.

Your sadness is also increased by reflecting on the words I speak to your soul, not for you, but for all. But do not refuse to receive them. I have so few people in the whole wide world who strain to hear my Word! The ones I would like to speak to, to lead them back onto the way of Life do not want to listen to Me. I then speak to the few who want to listen to Me. When it is useful, what I have said to my faithful secretly will be made known, and the Word will thus continue to resound in the world.

Do not elude my work, then, whatever it may be. Do not boast about it and do not be afraid of it. Let Me act. I never do anything without a purpose. Always come to Me with that confidence which is so pleasing to Me. When I find a confident soul, I open my Heart and enclose her within it. Do you think that anything which is real evil can happen to you if you are enclosed in my Heart? Why, not even Hell can harm you as long as you are there. And you'll be there as long as you are pure, loving, confident, and faithful" (p. 70-71).

So those of you who are pretty certain that you are here to serve, I welcome you. I accept you under that level of training and commitment and know you will grow more and more into the instruments of the Christ for suffering humanity. Those who are not as sure as I have outlined, please pray to Jesus and Mary to give you the experience and awareness of your purpose on this earth. Ask them to show you how you can be of service and what God's vision is for you and your work on earth. Tell them you are frightened or scared, but ask them to come and make you worthy of following them and doing God's will here.

Those on the spiritual path who have converted know what it means and how it feels. They would not wish for any other life. They find it difficult to relate to those who are on the fence wondering what they should do with their life. It is inconceivable that a soul would not want to express the way God wanted them to. But have compassion for the turmoil that your brothers and sisters are going through in their time of trial and test. Pray for them. Make your lives such an example of love and benevolence that they begin to praise God for you also because God's mercy and kindness is radiating through you. Hold each person in loving embrace, bathing them in the light of Christ. Even if you are persecuted for your love and gifts of grace, continue to heap coals of love on the heads of all your brothers and sisters. Jesus and Mary perpetually love this way. They have called you to the same purity and consistency of love. Each soul is a child of God waiting for a midwife to aid in their birth of coming into being sons and daughters of God.

Jesus and Mary have so much work to do on the earth. There is so little time and so many souls to reach with the healing light of Christ. There are so few disciples who have devoted their lives to Jesus and Mary and the work of God on the earth. The more powerful each of us is in our dedication and commitment, the more others will be drawn. How can souls be drawn if you still worry and are in doubt about your mission in life? It is true that some people will be repelled and angry that you are so sure of yourself. But the world does not change by cowardice, but by courage. Be courageous. Suffer the onslaught of negative opinions and rely totally on God within you. God is your source of supply and the rock of your salvation.

I pray over your souls. I hold each of you in my prayers and make sacrifices daily on your behalf. I ask the great Being of God to examine you and show up in you any places that are not converted. I ask Jesus and Mary to help each person be strong in their faith and be fully convinced that Jesus Christ and Mother Mary are real and are actually present and powerful in our world. Come to the Christ and be healed. Come and serve the hungry ones. Come and let the powers of the Creator move through you unhindered and without worldly considerations. Be fully Christed on your journey of service.

Chapter Five

The Transformative Path

We are a transformative path. We are not just a group of people who like to hang out and have similar ideas. That would make us just like every other religious organization. Following this path will really change you. When you have touched into peace, when you have risen into the presence of God and really had your heart broken by love, you will be very different, in a real way, from most people in the world who have not had that experience yet.

A transformative inner path is the process of having the things that are not useful to God destroyed in you so that you can be more yourself. What is the real you? The real you does not have any problems. The real you does not take from others or demand that others take care of you. The real you focuses on what is important inside you and within other people. The outer things are not important. Your soul already knows this. Your outer ego is caught up in hundreds of considerations designed to disturb you. You would not have to change anything about you if your inner being expressed through your mind, body and emotions without any resistance. The word transform means the form has to move across (trans) to some other expression. The form, your vehicle, which is your human mind and body, has to allow the movement of the Holy Spirit and the energies of your soul to express. That is called transformation. You are fine in the divine part of you. In the God Self within you, there is no confusion, no depression, no anger, no pride and no fear. Those negative emotions form a crust of darkness covering your soul and these energies have to be consciously let go of in order for you to be clear enough and humble enough to take direction from God within you. This inner direction, the voice of God within, comes directly from the God Self and is perfect. Your ability to listen and hear is what usually needs a whole lot of work and practice.

Until you are connected to God inside, you are still ill to some degree. You are not normal yet because your body, mind and emotions have not aligned to the pole star of the Self inside and become one with it in function. There are still parts of you that do whatever they want to do and are not under any conscious control by your soul. Our path is transformative – and difficult. Jesus said, "The way is narrow that leads to life and few there are that travel that way. Broad is the way that leads to destruction and many go that way" (Matthew 7:13). Most people go down the broad way and do not choose to discipline themselves in any way. They indulge themselves with whatever they whimsically feel in the moment without concerning themselves about the consequences or the effect it will have on them. In fact, many people are experiencing their conscience shutting down and getting sleepy as they slip into unconscious robotic motions and decisions. Most people are driven by fears and desires that they have never scrutinized or questioned. In this hazy existence, is it any wonder that so many crimes are committed? How can people consider each other compassionately if they are half-asleep?

A transformative path necessitates having actual experiences of changing from one expression to another and from one way of feeling, thinking and seeing to another more spiritual one. If there is no change in how you think, feel and move, then no transformation has occurred yet. The profound thing about this spiritual path is that you change and are refashioned into how God sees you. You start to become more alive. You feel more loving and peaceful. You find yourself less scattered and torn, more steady and caring. You see more how you can be useful and helpful to others. Since you experience fewer problems and concerns about yourself, you are in a better position to lend a hand and help others, even if it is simply a kind word or praying for their betterment. This is not a path of wishful thinking. It is not a path of reading the words of other saintly people. It is not a head path where you feed your head interesting tidbits warmed over but undigested. It is not a path of speculating or wallowing in lukewarm beliefs. There is no transformation available in a discussion group or a reading group, because there is only speculation about what the author or teacher meant when he said or wrote those things. Actually having a teacher present who can help you see what is real makes all the difference. This may be hard to accept; people are so jaded by not having any real experience that they assume no one else has any real experience of light or love or God. They are so fearful that someone might actually know something, that they will do practically anything to make sure what they read and hear is tentative. They refuse to believe that actually knowing something is possible.

A real spiritual path puts you through something. When you react to what the priest or teacher is saying, you should ask yourself if what they are saying scares you or stretches you. If it stretches you, then you should thank God for that. If it scares you, then you should examine your fears and find out if you were looking for a place where you did not have to give anything of yourself or change anything about yourself. If you do not want to change and do not want to grow, you are in the wrong place. Just listening to us will put you through things. We are dedicated to change this earth and change the hearts and minds of people. We are not going to be easy. We are not going to be cushy and fluffy. That would be almost impossible for us to do since it would scrape against how

Jesus and Mary teach and what they have held up as our mission on this planet.

If you had not left your connection and love for God, you would not be in the shape you are in. That is what we all find ourselves in when we come into incarnation. We are lost, separate and alone. You might have had parents, but they were mostly checked out and struggling with their own issues. So you find yourself a little lost when you arrive and not so warmly greeted and welcomed. Then after you get a little less mad, you look for a supportive spiritual community where there is some growth happening. Then the trouble begins because your fears come up very powerfully around whether you can trust anyone or trust the leaders. In time, you let a little love in and your heart breaks and you open to being taught. Some of you have not decided to let us teach you yet in a formal kind of way. Some of you are dancing outside the fire and it feels a little separate and disconnected. But you can come in if you want. You can choose to enter into the transformative process of love and get yourself hooked up to the source.

If you let us teach you, you are actually letting us love you. They are the same. We see you. We know what to do to heal you and we see your work ahead of you that you will need to do in order to become yourself. You have a couple of years of letting go to do and couple of years of taking on your new life in order to be completely changed. You can have such transformation and regeneration. It is yours for the asking. We do not even charge anyone for our training. The price you have to pay is the laying down of your life for your friends. The price is that you have to give up all your problems. You can no longer get mileage out of being separate and defended against closeness with your brothers and sisters.

It starts with light. God started with "Let there be light" in the beginning when creation began. Then that light vibrated at the frequency that God envisioned and that vibrating light produces life. Life was the movement in God's being after things were started. Then the life manifested and love held it all together and nurtured and supported the creation. With your own process, you need the conception of light in the baptism as your first spiritual initiation on the path. Then as you work with the teachings and with spiritual exercises, you will be brought to the experience of the sacrament of illumination.

Illumination is the second conscious spiritual initiation. The Eastern path would call this enlightenment. The illumination occurs under the watchful instigation of one of the Master's priests who are trained to prepare a student for this experience. The student must be prepared through various spiritual exercises and through the study of the New Testament and Tree of Life lessons. If the student is afraid of people, it will be hard to come into the illumination because he or she will fear the closeness of contact that they must have with the one teaching them. If you cannot trust a teacher, then you are not going to relax while they are working on you or guiding you. The illumination takes place when your outer person lets go and lets God. You have relaxed into God and God's love sufficiently so that the light of Christ builds up a great charge of light in the body. At this point the priest will seal the light in the flesh body so that you can see the light in your body when the room is completely dark. This light will show up everything in you that is real and also those things that are not real. Each initiation is a beginning where you take on the energies that have been given to you in the experience.

Jesus says in *The Notebooks 1943*:

> "You are always mine until love is dead in you. And it is for the wounded children that I gave my Blood. Be just, then, and merciful to yourselves, as I am. Strive to know me and love me so as not to deprive your souls of their right to eternal joy.

> Get back onto the way of Life. My commandments are that way. Seek to bear them in mind during the day. For if weakness then drags you into slight errors, I assure you that you should not be demoralized over it.

Tomorrow you will do better than today, and the day after tomorrow, better than tomorrow. A plant grows slowly. Every day a new little root, every day a new leaf. But how beautiful it is when it has grown! Perfection is like this, children. It is conquered by degrees.

But what do you think – that I will give a lesser reward to those who did not reach the maximum immediately? No, on the contrary, between those who were holy by my grace and those who wanted to be holy against their nature, I will gaze with eyes twice as loving at this hero of love. The reward in eternity is one alone: the vision of God. But the initial embrace of union between the combatants who are victorious over the flesh, the world and the devil – in whom throughout life the latter agitated their serpentine essence, cut off a thousand times and rising again a thousand times – shall be powerful, with a special ecstasy.

I tell you so. Believe Me, the Truth. How urgent is the need for that memory in you now! You die from not remembering to be Christians. Turn to Christ. Wisdom says, 'And those who turned to that sign were not healed by what they saw, but by You, the Savoir of all.

That's it, O children. You are not healed of your individual and public infirmities because you are unable to see me. Practices do not count; reprisals create vaster evil; acts of vengeance kill those committing them before those enduring them; the shelters fall without sheltering you. But if you came to Me, you would be saved. In regard to the life of this earth, and that of the hereafter.

I repeat my wish. Let many acts of adoration be offered to the Cross, which is the throne of power of Jesus, your Savior. As the serpent raised up on the cross had the power to heal the Jews, so I, the One who is immortal, raised up on the Cross, will have the power to set to flight what frightens and torments you, for I am the Lord of life and death and can place life where death is already imminent and overcome death by calling back to life.

No one, except Me, can do this. Satan can give you all powers, but not that of calling back vital movement. On the contrary, he teaches you to shatter lives with hatred for the Giver of life, who, to nourish you not only for bodily life, for which He has grain germinate and form ears, but for spiritual life, gives you the Bread which the angels adore because it is the Flesh of the Son of God. He gives it to you, not asking for anything in exchange except love and faith, and, indeed, like a holy Beggar asks you to receive Him into yourselves, for He makes being with you his joy.

In you that Bread is transformed into Life and Grace; it is transformed into Salvation, Light, Joy and Wisdom. You become all when you are an all with the Son of God. The Word of the Father speaks softly when He remains like a heart in your breast. And it is my Word that conserves for Eternal Life those who do not forswear their supernatural filiation" (p. 460-461).

Light is the Solution

N ewer students and members of our spiritual communities sometimes think that when we speak of experiencing the light in our bodies, it is metaphorical or merely symbolic. Our ministers teach about the light filling the body and keeping the eye single so that the whole body will be full of light; yet many do not register in heart and mind what this means. Carrying light within seems so different than the fears and negative tendencies that most people experience all week long. Many people have secret fears of being found out to be very negative and full of faults. Some worry about being discovered to have so much wrong with them that they think they could never deserve such a gift from God as having light in their flesh and consciousness.

The light is a blessing from God to every human being that gets out of the way and opens to receive it. Communion is powerful way to receive God's blessing, which many people are familiar with. It is a complete gift of Jesus, Mary and God. Communion is the start of a connection to the grace and love of God who made you. The light is the same thing. God wants you back in union with God. God knows your weaknesses and has taken into consideration your problems and still presents you with the means to be close and feel the love that God pours out for you. The love of God makes all these gifts possible, but you have to open yourself to receive. If you start taking a gift and you tell God how miserable you are and how unworthy you are and how hard it is to accept, what is God going to do? God might see that you are not able to receive anything because you are spending most of your time convincing God that you do not deserve and cannot carry the gift with gratitude and acceptance.

The three aspects or qualities of God are light, life and love. In the beginning of creation when God spoke the creative word, light shone in the darkness and the darkness was confounded and fled before its majesty. Then the light increased, causing a quickening of vitality and vibration that produced life. This life flowed through all of creation, supporting and invigorating everything and moving everything along in its progress. From the life, love came to support, hold and foster more of the same. This is a natural progression for everyone who opens to God and wants to come back into union with God. What is required is that you stop judging yourself and imagining you can evaluate anything adequately. You are not able to determine how far along you are spiritually. You are not even able to change one hair white or black, as Jesus said. And yet you scoreboard your badness and you tally your faults like you were proud of them. Instead you should be so tired of them that you are willing to sell them for even a small blessing of light, love and grace from God. Just to being able to feel the presence of God should be enough to give anything over and let it go.

When you stop looking outside yourself, you really start to grow spiritually. When you stop fearing evaluations from those in spiritual authority, such as priests or teachers, when you cease inventorying your deficits, then you begin to have experiences of grace and love. Looking outside yourself means you are comparing the blessings others receive with what scraps and crumbs you have been given. Looking outside yourself means you are thoroughly distracted in the issues of your ego trying to stack up against all the other people you are watching to make sure you are not as bad or a little better than them. Looking outside is seeing a goal that your ego and head have determined would indicate that you were doing fine, and you shoot for that. You see how tiresome and meaningless that is? You cannot figure anything out in terms of your spiritual progress, so why do you waste your time on those kinds of meaningless things? You are a soul that has God inside. Inside you, you are fine and nothing needs to be done. God resides there waiting for the outer you to stop resisting God's light and love.

The lights have to turn on in your being and emanate through your soul into your mind, heart and body so that you can really see and know the truth. You cannot really know anything or see anything truly without light. Light is necessary in order for your life to be regenerated. Light is spiritual and internal. There is some reflection in the outer world of actual physical light, but the real experience of light comes from within, from God. When the outer person really lets go and lets God, there are forces within the soul that bring about instantaneous illumination of the outer person. Will you please let go? Will you stop looking outside yourself? Will you stop being jealous and comparing, or even imagining you have the capacity to compare correctly where you are with where someone else is? That is the job of priests and teachers.

Another necessary feature of being able to come into the experience of the light or illumination is that you trust a spiritual teacher and allow them to address those things in you that are in the way of the light. For example, if you have darkness that you listen to or that has been comforting you, then you will be blocking the light. If you have addictions and faults that you know are bad for you and you do not do anything about them, then that impurity in you will block the light. Those places in you that you are attached to self-comfort, that are negative and filled with darkness, are areas where you are playing God and have actually evicted God. To allow those tendencies and expressions to be in you is a choice. You choose them or they would not be there. Your choosing them is a statement that you are too scared to let them go and trust that God will take care of you. In other words, you are not at the place where you will let God in to take care of you and love you and guide you. You need to change that and start trusting the God who made you. God knows you even if you only know God as a concept. God loves you even if you only feel a false and meager and slimy love for yourself. God's love is pure and perfect and powerful. Compared to God's, your love is pathetic until you let that perfect love in.

You have to have light or you cannot see other people or yourself. You will not know where you are going. You will trip and fall many times since you have chosen to walk in darkness. When a person does not know and yet still walks in darkness, they trip and make mistakes. When a person who carries light trips and falls, they need to get right back up and change and not look back to continually criticize themselves, to energetically beat themselves up. You cannot move along the spiritual path by beating yourself up. No good can come from flailing away and ripping hunks of flesh off of yourself. Your violence to yourself has to stop. That is not love and it is not constructive. You have to start to let love in and that means you have to turn over the job of correcting you and healing you to a spiritual teacher. It is pride that thinks you are so good at criticizing. You are not good at it and often you criticize things that deserve compassion.

You attack things in yourself that are good at the core because you are blinded by your own darkness. You cannot see clearly until you have light. That does not just mean receiving the sacrament of illumination, because it will take many years to turn into a completely lighted being. Even if you have been illumined, you have to appreciate it and cultivate it, or you will not continue to grow in light.

The title "Light is the Solution" presupposes a problem. Lack of light is the problem. Lack of light in you makes you spiritually blind. Lack of light in your flesh makes the desires of the body and its prejudices tear you to pieces. Lack of light makes a home for the demons and allows all the seven departments of evil to live in you. Asking for God's light to be in you starts the tumultuous process of dissolving those patterns of darkness that have troubled you so thoroughly. This Christ light is a grace and benevolence of God that comes to heal your body, mind, heart and soul. Staying in the light continues the regeneration and makes possible an inner environment where God can reside and express through you. How can God act in you when a thousand crushing impurities shut out the light? How can God speak through your lips when your tongue speaks false words in lies, conceits and deceits? When will you choose light over darkness? When will you ask for help from Jesus and Mary to enlighten you and keep you from all destructive patterns and from darkness? When a soul makes that choice with no desire to turn back to old ways of anger, fear and pride, then we say that that person has converted completely to God and light.

Even people who have received the illumination have to soak in the light to teach the bodily cells to change over to a new consciousness. Anything worthwhile takes work and effort. Anything lasting needs constant attention and love. To carry the light and to grow that light within your being, you have to spend time with it. It is like how babies grow. At first you need plenty of time, lots of attention and a fairly rigorous feeding schedule every two hours. The old consciousness must be trained to allow more and more light into the flesh, emotions and mind. In this way, the dark past is shown up in the light and the light makes those patterns uncomfortable because they are so incompatible. This painful shedding of old ways shows you how far you had drifted from purity and love. You went away out of willfulness and sorrow, sometimes anger and shame. When you went away, it was not long before you were not aware how far you had strayed from love and from light. You were too numb and blind to know how lost you were and how much sin covered you. It took God's love and light to break you out of the mud so you could feel the movement of life again. Remember, light brings life. Life is what happens after light takes place.

Our students who have experienced the illumination are asked to review how much light they see and how often they think of the light. They do serious work at dosing their bodies in light to make the cells absorb more and more light. When the light increases in your body, your sight will clear and you will be able to discern more easily between things of God and things that are not of God. When you walk into a room, your light will shine so that what is happening in the room shows up the truth. When you put your hands on anything, you can feel and see light move into the objects you touch. When you clean something, the love of God and the Christ light move into the substance of the object so that the light resides and stays with that object. This explains why some homes carry a presence of love and peace and others have chaos and negative energy. In one house there is love and light and in the other there is anger, fear, worry and hatred. The energy of those emotions and thoughts enter the very cells of the walls and paint and contaminate that house. We have all felt almost nauseous in a home like that, whereas in a house where people love and are peaceful, we feel uplifted and blessed being there.

> "…come to the Light of the world, that your houses may be bright with light. I bring you the Light. Nothing else. I have no riches and I do not promise worldly honours. But I possess all the supernatural wealth of My Father and I promise the eternal honour of Heaven to those who will follow God with love and charity" (*The Poem of the Man-God*, Vol. 1, p. 416).

Chapter Seven

The Life of a Lighted Being

What is it like to have light in your body? It is like a quickening stream of exhilarating power moving in your veins. Having the light in your cells causes a vibratory lift of your consciousness and moves great power in your body. The light vivifies and renews the flesh and causes it to change its quality to one of effervescent radiance. Dense flesh does not shine, because it is atrophying. It is getting denser and thicker by the law of karma. You are either making yourself denser and more earthly in your senses and cells or you are making your cells more of the nature of light and heaven. When a person does not have much light, they are slowly getting more like their animal body, more sinewy and leathery. The light from the soul is not able to move from within them out into their flesh with the Godly radiance of divinity. The ego and outer consciousness, being so focused on what is transitory and meaningless, shuts down the light and prevents it from shining through the spiritual body into the physical body. Without the revitalizing power of the light, the flesh loses its vibrancy and ability to regenerate.

In the average human being's lifespan one's energy tends to move from vibrant as a child to animated as an adolescent to powerful as a young adult and gradually more and more rigid as aging occurs; people coast to the finish line sick and suffering from a serious illness. Getting ill is an accepted practice in the West as a way to exit from this lifetime. It is amazing that people demonstrate very little courage in accepting death when it is their time to go. Dying smoothly and gracefully when it is time to go should be the natural way of death. How many people die gracefully after a life well lived? How many leave their bodies having a conscious knowledge of God? How many die on the earth with any degree of light in their flesh or any trusting hope in a continuous life? Most people die terrified because they have almost no experience of God and no light in their body or consciousness. They have done very little work on themselves and are virtually unprepared for life in the spiritual world.

Having light in your body is the difference between one who is dead or dying and one who is alive with life. Being truly alive means God's energy is moving through you unencumbered, unrestricted. God is light. Where there is no light, God cannot be present. The light shows things up as I said before, and it also brings healing to parts of you that need to be healed, raised up and brought into balance. Because the light is intelligent, the light knows what to do inside you, if you let it shine throughout your being.

If you have light in your body, you will wake up each day and give glory to God for creating you: all the intelligence, life, energy, beauty and gifts in you are given by God. You will be grateful and loving to God for these things. With the light in you, you will be growing into more of your true nature and lighter all the time. Your intelligence will more closely reflect God's intelligence because there is no intelligence outside God. Healing energies will flow through as you go about your day, and inspirations will come to you about how to improve things and what to create in your world. You will look at things, and since you can keep your mind focused on one thing, you will be able to see clearly what is real. You will have less and less darkness in your life because you have dedicated yourself to the Light. Egotism is darkness. Selfishness and anger are darkness. Pride and arrogance are darkness. Fear and worry are darkness. These attitudes cannot exist in the light as they are so different from the nature of the light. Light is healing, open, warm, loving, and respectful of other people. Light brings the best out in people and makes them creative. Light opens the heart and lets love move to and from people. Light makes it possible for you to see where you are going and what is of God and what is not. Light gives true discrimination. We often meet people who have no idea what they are doing or why they are doing it. This is because they have no Light in them and are unable to really discern what is real and true from what is not. They are blind people wandering around the earth pretending to know things, as they spout their pseudo-knowledge aimed to impress other people. But because they have no light, they can only lead people away from God. That kind of unenlightened voice is what most people listen to and follow in this world.

A person with the light devotes their energies to what God wants them to do. In the light, God begins to educate you to what needs to be done and how things are to be handled. The light will show up the flaws in your schemes and plans and lead you into the right way of doing things. There is a way of light and a way of darkness. You cannot have both. You cannot have it your way and God's way at the same time. You have to choose. If you care, you have to choose.

Most people are still trying to develop something unique in order to get attention from other people. Most people are working on presenting some trait of character or some talent or skill that will impress other people, instead of just being yourself. Who are you really? What is your true nature? Wouldn't you have to go to the Source of All in order to find the blueprint of the original design by the great Architect? Why wouldn't you want to know what that is? Are you still so jaded by the initial wounds of your parents that you can't trust anyone anymore? Do you want to carry that anger around with you and inflict it on everyone you meet for the rest of your days? I don't think you do. I think you want to heal and be well now. You are probably striving to know who you are, or you wouldn't be reading this book. So with that in mind, let's find out what the great architect had in mind when God created you. Learn to ask inside what your true nature really is and let go of and give up any ideas about how to be special or original. You can't make yourself better. You can't dream up becoming someone people will really love, unless you want to be twisted and distorted and wind up in a heap of trouble. Most people are so full of entangled desires and misperceptions that they barely can recognize any of their inherent divinity any longer. I know you can mouth the words that you are a child of God. I know your head can tell you many beautiful sayings and trite mental comfort foods. But very people really know anything for sure. I am not putting you down. I am asking you to humble yourself to the truth of what you really know.

What do you know for sure? What is totally clear to you about God and yourself? That is the starting point. Don't jack it up or puff it up. Just be honest and simple. It is not a great problem if you don't know certain things. It is a huge problem if you think you do and you really don't. So the baseline is what you are sure of, and the rest we can teach you. But I have to warn you that most of what you think you are is a severe mental misconception that keeps you from getting to know yourself, and keeps you from the light and knowing God. You have to unlearn so many things. You have to divest yourself of so much silliness and craziness, most of which you have created yourself, and some of which was put on you by your caregivers. You have to bend your knees a little or you will not be able to experience God. You will be too full of fear and defensiveness that you really are the flawed person that other people have said you are. You will be too proud to accept the fact that you only know what you know and you need to experience the rest. You will have to be honest about the fact that if you could have attained the experience of the illumination of the light of Christ by your own efforts, you would have done so. But you have had no guide, no one who had the experience themselves to take you there. Most of you have had pseudo-guides who gave you warmed over scraps, platitudes designed to stroke your ego, which keeps you from arriving at the real experience. That means it doesn't work. If you are going to allow yourself to be flattered, then you deserve not to know the true experience of God and the light. If you are satisfied with clever answers and superficial truths, then you are not ready for what is real.

If this is biting a little or bruising your ego, imagine what it is going to be like if you hear the deeper teachings. Get used to being shown the truth about yourself or you won't be able to go within to find God. God is no respecter of persons. In other words, God made you and knows how far you have strayed from the way God wanted you to be. Real spiritual teachers want you the way God made you, not some aberration puffed up with arrogant pride or false teachings. They want to heal you of the mistakes of your past. They want you to have the courage to go through the purification of your desire nature, the transformation of your thinking process and the regeneration of your flesh body. They know what to do because their own teachers taught them well. Everyone is in a process of perfecting and becoming more and more light. In time, there will be no darkness at all in you because of the generosity and love of your teachers. If you want to grow, this is what to do: let a real spiritual teacher know you. Let them grow you. Let them in to all the crevices, nooks and crannies of your life so they can heal your world. There is no relationship more close and intimate and real than with your teachers. You will find the love you received as a child only a pale and insufficient reflection of what love you can expect.

If you are holding on to relationships from the past, let them go. Trying to get love out of people who don't really know how to love, such as parents, spouses, or family, is like trying to squeeze blood out of a turnip. Go ahead and try, but you will receive as little or less than you did back then. Go ahead and try. Actually, haven't you been trying for many years to receive what you demanded and expected from them? If you are philosophical and think you are beyond all that, as some of you pridefully feel, then what happens to you in a love relationship? Don't you make a valiant attempt to train the lucky partner to repair all the damage of the former pain suffered from your parents? Don't you project all your expectations on the partner to take care of everything that was missed in earlier life? You better believe you do. That means you did not let it go and you did not forgive and you did not heal from those wounds, or you would not act them out again on the unlucky victim you choose as a partner. I pray that you understand there will never be any fulfilling relationship with another human being unless and until you establish and maintain your relationship with God.

Holding onto the past prevents the light. Indicting God for all the pain you have experienced in life also blocks the light. Making sure you are safe behind the walls of your castle with sentinels guarding the gates will not help you. Letting yourself love other people and disciplining yourself to stop thinking about yourself and your hurts will move you into a completely different life.

> "Do you perhaps want to deceive yourselves by telling yourselves that it is only an earthly necessity which spurs you to do your will, but at the heart you would like to do God's because you prefer it? Hypocrites, hypocrites, hypocrites.

> In you is a judge that knows no sleep, and it is your spirit. Even if you mortally wound it and condemn it to perish, it cries out in you, as long as you are on this earth, shouting its heavenly anguish. You weigh it

down and gag it to make it immobile and mute, but it tosses and turns until getting free of your gag and hurls its cry into the desolate silence of your hearts. And, like the cry of my Forerunner, John the Baptist, that voice is vexing for you so that you try to squelch it forever. You will never be able to. As long as you live, you will hear it, and in the hereafter it will shout louder, reproaching you for your crime as killers of your souls.

The key to certain human aberrations which grow and grow and lead the individual to monstrous misdeeds lies in this voice of conscience, which you try to numb with new bounds of ferocity, just as people who have taken poison try to forget their deliberate misfortune by poisoning themselves more and more, to the point of hebetude.

Be sons and daughters, my creatures. Love – love our good Father who is in Heaven. Love Him as much as you can. It will then be easy for you to follow His blessed will and make yourselves a destiny of eternal glory" (*The Notebooks 1943*, p. 319).

Chapter Eight

I Want to Give You the Light

I want to give you the light. This light is not a mental concept or some nice idea. In all spiritual schools and traditions, the enlightenment or illumination is one of the goals of their spiritual practice. On the inner path of the Order of Christ/Sophia, it is our mission to bring the light of Christ to each person who dedicates to prepare for it. It is not like giving someone a mantra to say over and over to themselves while they still their mind. It is not a magical password that brings you into some special knowledge that others do not have. It is not a trick of the brain. It is not attained by some strenuous breathing exercise or difficult yoga position. Attaining the light of Christ is only arrived at by experiencing that light and following the directions of your teachers.

As John says in the Gospel, "This is the light that illumines everyone that comes into the world." It is the birth of the light in the cells of your flesh. This light is a luminous glow of fire and radiance that shines forth from within the center of your inner Being, the God Self. From the God Self, there radiates the intense light of the Christ that will shine easily within and around you if you relax and give over to God. When you truly dedicate yourself to be a vehicle for the presence of God, and devote yourself to that striving, then soon the dawn of the light comes as an experience that destroys the dark of night. The darkness you lived in before this experience is comprised of all of the sadness, pain, fear, pride, misconception and anger that human beings wallow in. The illumination is the second of the three great initiations on the spiritual path. The first is the baptism where the seed of light is planted in your physical/spiritual consciousness, and you work to nurture that seed until it is delivered at the birth of the light. You nurture the light by receiving communion, by studying the New Testament and the life of Jesus and Mary, and by your work with your teacher and doing the spiritual exercises and meditations that are given to you for your growth. Receiving communion is a tremendous gift to you that you can have every morning, if you have the time and the discipline, where you will be given a free gift of the cleansing and clarifying body and blood of a God. As you receive this life within you, you are changed imperceptibly at first, and many of your errors and difficulties are lifted from you right there at communion. Your troubles are transformed without your doing very much at all, because it is the love of our masters who give that to you freely.

After the introductory classes, students come to realize there is a lot more they can learn and be participating in with our order. They learn to ask a priest to teach them, and this begins the conscious spiritual path. The teacher takes them through a retrospection of their past and prepares them for baptism. The baptism is a baptism into Christ and not into the order or a spiritual school. It is the beginning of a conscious relationship with Jesus and Mary as your direct teachers. Through Jesus and Mary, your earthly teachers – deacons or priests – take you on and are responsible for watching over your soul as you grow and develop as disciples. They are devoted entirely to the growth of souls on this planet. The deacons must have come into the experience of the illumination or they would not be able to really serve. How could you lead others if you were not able to see? If you did not have the interior light radiating inside you and shining out, how could you see where you are going, much less guide anyone else along the path? Our priests are all Self-Realized and know God within themselves. That is the only way the true priesthood can function successfully. So you begin your active training with your teacher who will prepare you and baptize you.

After the baptism you go through lots of changes and adjustments. You sometimes go into pretty dark places, just as Jesus was led by the spirit out into the wilderness to be tempted by the adversary. This happens to every person on the spiritual path. It does not happen the afternoon after the baptism as some have thought, but it usually happens within the first few weeks or months from the time of the baptism. The adversary is the part of you that holds on to the patterns that have worked in the past and kept you safe when you did not realize there was God. When you were afraid and alone and people were hurting you, the adversary was built up in you as a way to survive while you were unaware of your divine nature. It has a strong voice in you and will try to convince you to stay the way you have always been. Any movement towards God is seen as threatening to the adversary. So during this process you are taught to recognize its voice and the fears and pride that support it, while you are moving toward being a god being.

The baptism plants the seed, the conception of light in your body and consciousness. Remember, your soul knows God and is in touch with the Creator all the time, but your mind, emotions and body are not. Most people have that awareness and connection shut down by the time they are four years old. Sometimes it is the parents and sometimes the education by everyone else in society. If the parents are not consciously striving to be sons and daughters of God, how can they possibly expect their children to connect or be interested in God? So the outer form – the body, mind and emotions – has to be changed by the action of the spiritual practices, in order to find God within. As you stay connected to the teachings and your teacher during this process, you can stand greater and greater Presence of God in your body. You can feel more life moving through you. You are allow-

ing more healing energy to move through you during blessing groups, communion and meditations. You might notice
changes in your skin, in the tension of your mind and the
cells of your body. Your health starts to adjust because of the
peace that you are permitting to enter into you. The changes
are subtle at first and then more earth-shaking. As you are
faithful in doing the spiritual exercises you are given, you are
disciplining that most unruly mind of yours and beginning
to be able to tell when you are out of balance and when you
are in accord. You are then asked to begin working with light
exercises to flood your body with light.

At some point the teacher asks you to look for the Light
within. Your mind goes numb, and you feel denser than ever
because you have no idea what the teacher is talking about.
You look inside in meditation and see practically nothing
for a little while because it is such a different direction for
your focus. Then you start to see some light within you, and
you check your eyes to make sure you are not imagining
things. As you are maintaining contact on a regular basis
with the teacher, you share what you are experiencing and
the teacher guides you to let go of your body consciousness
and mental concepts in order to allow more and more light
into your flesh body. Gradually the light increases and when
it has grown quite strong and full, you are prepared for the
illumination. A priest in our order can bring you into the
illumination. They will do this in a sacramental form in our
chapels and will seal the light of Christ into the cells of your

flesh. Then you are said to be illumined and carry the light of Christ in your body.

We call baptism, illumination and Self-realization the three great solar initiations because they are the three initiations that bring a soul into consciousness atonement with God. Each initiation initiates you into a new beginning and so is only the first step to taking on that particular new experience. It will take much work and assimilation to come into the full illumination after you receive the light. Since it is a beginning, there is much to be learned and much to take on. You will continue to do light exercises to increase the light and bathe your whole being in the light. The process continues until you evolve to the point where there is so much light, your body is a light veil over your real nature, the soul. As the physical body increases with more and more light, your whole being is healed and your very cells change and become more spiritual. Your spiritual sight is opened and you are able to affect the world around you to a much greater degree. You are growing in purity, because there is no light without purification. During the process of attaining the light and afterwards when it is increasing within you, the light is showing up things of a negative nature. You are purging those things that are dark because the light cannot exist where there is darkness and darkness flees before the advancement of the light. In God there is no darkness at all, so only where God is not, can there be darkness. The only place darkness can exist is where a human or created consciousness separates from their Creator and creates darkness. God cannot will evil and cannot violate God's own nature, which is light.

Living in the light takes courage because the light shows up anything that is not God. Everything false, tricky, mean, underhanded and negative is shown up in the light. The selfishness, pride and fear which are at the base of all darkness are magnified so you can see it and understand it. Then you can make a decision that you don't want these kinds of things in your life. When you are illumined, you are a living source of light for all around you. The light shines as much as you let it and as much as you get conscious of directing it. The light goes where you place your attention and so in the direction of your attention, things show up for what they are. People around you feel the presence of the light even if they do not actually see it, and they get blessed by it. They might react to that light or may want to get away from you. But at least, you know that is what happens to people when they decide they don't want things to be shown up as they are. They still want to hide and will hate to get anywhere near the Light. The light is intelligent and has an intimate connection to the source where the light comes from, which is God.

The light acts on your glands and blood and lymph, producing a cleansing purging energy. Anything that is stressed will be released as the light increases and continues its action in the body. The light changes your appetites and desires. The raging tempest of your emotions must be tamed and subdued by working with the light and continuing your spiritual exercises, meditations and classes. Communion takes on a whole new significance as you feel more the presence of Jesus and Mary as you receive their body and blood. You are taking in, in manageable doses, the pure love of God through the communion. Your consciousness and body are changed by this. You can hear the teachers and priests in a whole new dimension, on a whole new level, because your spiritual sight has been opened so much more. You understand so many of the spiritual teachings that everything becomes simpler and easier to understand.

With the receiving of the light comes another cleansing that is a little troubling. As Paul says in Hebrews 10:32, "But recall those earlier days when, after you had been illuminated, you endured a hard struggle with sufferings." The darkness shows up much more in the light. The faults and character defects, the weakness and bad habits, the hiding and games show up so much in the light that it can become a little uncomfortable. But it is a necessary part of the process of spiritual development, and you need to be courageous and strong in facing these not so attractive aspects of yourself. You don't become instantly perfect with the receiving of the light of Christ, so you need to be patient with the process, and confident of help from Jesus and Mary as you move through to perfection. Jesus said, "Be perfect, as your Father-Mother is perfect." That means it is possible. So you have to strive to be perfect, or you will never get there. The light purifies, cleanses and regenerates, and each part of the process is vital to your future growth as a disciple of Christ. It took the Apostles three years to arrive at being fairly perfect. They had to fail and be broken of their pride, ego and their false self-centered confidence. When they were encouraged and forgiven by Jesus for their humanness, they became heroic in love with the gifts of the spirit flowing through them.

In our order, students receive the illumination at the earliest time that is safely possible for them to receive this gift. We do not hold back unless there is some serious negative tendency that the student has to let go of before they can receive. Sometimes the negative tendencies you are holding onto become a block to receiving the light, and this is the reason it can't be given to you. You might have another god that you find more attractive. We then wait for you to grow tired of your false god until you demonstrate your devotion to the one true God. Jesus said, "If your eye is single, your whole body will be filled with light." This single eye is when you keep your whole consciousness on becoming a lighted vessel for God, when your whole attention is devoted to knowing God and being like God. God is light, and shines like the sun. That is your nature.

Chapter Nine

Learning to Love Yourself

When we hear the word "love" we are struck by a myriad of images. Love conjures up feelings of romantic interactions, the heartfelt protection and celebration for our children or some passionate embrace. Those are expressions of love if they come from the heart and are not demanding, pushy, controlling or suffocating. But what is love really? Where does it come from and how does it work? Is it a contagious disease that only some people are lucky enough to acquire? I think that the way love is presented to us in the media and TV makes it out to be a random event that might happen to anyone if they are in the right place and with the right person. Infatuation and attraction have very little to do with love and often do not travel very well together. Attraction is the ignition in a relationship while love is the real engine that is much deeper.

I don't want to talk very much about how people fall or rise in love, because then we would be adding another person to our topic beside ourselves. I want to talk about the way love works or does not work inside of you, without talking about another person.

Inside of each one of us is a radiant center of love residing in the soul. There is tremendous power and activity inside our being that is constantly radiating and giving forth life, light, and love. This center of creativity and source of energy residing within us is ever in action and ever at rest. Without a real connection to the source of our inner being, we aren't able to truly love. If we are not sure of who we are, then who is doing the loving when we love someone? We have to be connected within to the deeper parts of ourselves in order to draw from the wellspring residing there. We can only love another person to the degree that we love ourselves. We can only love ourselves to the degree that we do not fear who we are.

Most people suffer the mythology that we need to find someone who will be all the things we don't think we are. We look for someone who can do all the things we may not be able to do, and someone who can carry for us those skills and abilities that we do not see in ourselves. This creates a tremendous problem of projection of those parts of ourselves that we have disowned onto the partner. If we come to relationship with those kinds of deficits and lacks, is it any wonder that there is so much conflict and turmoil in relationship? When we were little, say around four or five years of age, we internalized the rejection of our person and felt that we were not enough to handle the circumstances we faced. We were scared, angry, hurt, and worried by all of the events and personal interactions we experienced. Who was going to help us cope with these? When we looked around, no one was there who understood. Our conscious mind figured out ways to generate stability by using worried, angry, or fearful thoughts to handle the events we could not understand. Our ego compensated by building up a defense of pride and fear to counterbalance all the hurtful assaults on our person. We felt not seen, not heard, not known and not protected. Our conscious mind and ego built up stronger reactions and rituals of thought to handle the intensity of our loneliness. Soon we generated many quirky behaviors and mental concepts of safety and self-protection and these formed a wall of thoughts in our consciousness about what keeps us safe. Gradually, we trusted our own ideas more than the evidence of those who cared for us and we suffered the intense loneliness of one not understood, seen, or felt. We cut off our own feeling side and remained as sentinels on the tower of our own watchfulness. This condition grew until it was an impressive army of control agents in our consciousness, keeping us safe from assaults.

The result of this program of disconnectedness is that each of us lost touch with our true feelings. True feelings are not emotions. Emotions come from reactions from outside things and people. All emotions are negative. Emotions of anger, pride, over-sensitivity, fear, worry, irritability and sadness for oneself are always negative and reactive because they make an attempt to protect our survival at all costs. Real feelings are not reactive. They just are. They are a deep level of our being. A real feeling has its own integrity, its own space and does not need anything to verify it or console it. Real feeling is something quite deep within the psyche and is more you than anything else you have known. It is the place of peace, contentment, stillness, love, happiness, simplicity and joy. It can have sadness, but not the kind that turns into feeling sorry for yourself. That is a slippery slope, and slides quickly into feeling bad about yourself, and beating yourself up for things. Feelings are the most real part of you and very close to your soul. Since it is the most real part of you, it is usually the most repressed and confined because of all the wounding and hurtful things you have suffered.

We can teach you to discern the difference between emotions and feelings. Your head churns out the emotions to fake you out and fool you into thinking they are real feelings. They are mock feelings posing as feelings. Your head cannot really do any feeling at all; only your inner being and soul can feel. The head fools you into thinking you are unsafe; it scares you into protecting yourself. Then it controls you and keeps you in an agitated and hyper-alert state. In this stressful vigilance, it feigns helpfulness and sells you on how much you need your head to manage things. Actually, your head is a control freak and wants to power over you at any cost. It will lie, cheat and manipulate in order to stay in power. Over the years it gains more and more power by trickery and causing you to be insecure about yourself. If you listen to it long enough, you will lose your sense of who you really are. Most people have no idea what they really feel underneath the massive fears and insecurities they were sold by their thinking mind.

The only way to love yourself truly is to fire those negative voices and affirm the truth about you. You are good. That is the way you were created. You did not create yourself, so some being that was incredibly thoughtful and intelligent must have. Think accepting thoughts about yourself and affirm the way you want to be in your life. If you can love yourself, then you will, in proportion to your ability to do that, allow others to experience and love you. Be rebellious about the lies and square off with them until they back off. You are more powerful than the program you experienced growing up. Your life is more important than a few lies. There is nothing in the depths of your being that is anything else but good. The outer stuff is not really you, so let it go. Learn to love yourself.

When you go inside your feelings and let yourself feel what is important, you will find that it is very simple and clear.

There is no worry there. There is no anger or negative energy there. The real feelings are very close to your soul and the most important part of you. You have to shut up the negative head voices to go there, otherwise you will fall for some disturbance spewed out of the mind to get you off balance and scared again. You have to be intensely watchful that those thoughts of the mind have no power over you and are not allowed to interfere with what you truly care about. In the feelings, you will be able to know what you value, what means a great deal to you, and how you want to live. When you can value your feelings, you will be truly loving the real you. All problems resolve when you know what you are truly feeling.

Chapter Ten

Purification of the Soul

We come to earth as souls who have been in existence for eons of time. We do not start our existence in this one embodiment and do not cease to exist after we take off this coat at death. Birth and death are the passages but life is the whole journey of our developing divinity. If we have existed before each incarnation, then it stands to reason that we have experience as souls that is recorded and makes up who we are. These experiences become our developing personality much like adding filters over a camera lens changes the brightness and color of the light moving through a medium.

When people talk about soul, they talk about it as if it were this obelisk or icon of mystery. To many, the soul is this numinous something that seems impossible for them to describe and so awesome that people just go "wow." They wink at each other knowingly when they talk about soul, as if they understand something about it. It is much like when people speak of God and they kind of muse about how they would feel if there were such a being. It is hard for people to admit that they do not have any personal experience of soul, because they so much want to believe that they do have the experience or at least know enough to write books about it. Most of the books on the soul are just talking about a neat place to visit and how awesome it might be if one actually had a soul. They rarely talk about an experience of actually seeing the soul, much less knowing what the soul is. People are so intent on speaking about things they do not know and discussing things they only half understand.

Many of you have felt a center in your being that could easily resemble a description of soul. But you have to know that if you have not seen the soul and the God being within you, then you do not really know what the soul is. This level of honesty is going to be very important to your integrity as you move along the spiritual path. It is vital that you get the importance of being brutally honest about where you are and what you do and do not know. If you can be honest about what you have and have not experienced, you will have your humility intact and be in a better position to begin the process of discovering who you are. It will take much work to really know your soul.

Meditation is the main activity that will help you experience the soul. Only by going within and stilling that speculating mind of yours will you be able to be shown your own soul. There is a price to pay for that knowledge and that experience. You do not need to know the soul if you are caught up in the way other people think. If you are still trying to fit in with other people, you are not going to be able to understand your soul. If you still want to know what is acceptable and normal in the world, then you are not ready for experiencing your soul. Nothing that your mind or emotions can come up with will get you any closer to your soul. You will need humility and a great deal of spiritual muscle to arrive at the experience of your soul. You cannot just think about it and arrive at a well-sculpted description and be satisfied with that. That would be ridiculous and shallow. You cannot think your way into the experience of God or the soul. Only by being led by one who knows can you hope to attain this experience. This will involve you admitting that you do not know. You will have to ask for help. Then you will have to do what that guide or teacher asks you to do with the goal of experiencing your soul.

Jesus said in *The Poem of the Man-God*, Vol. 2:

> "You do not want to purify the waters of your souls, you prefer to be putrid filth. It does not matter. I do *My* duty as the Eternal Saviour" (p. 752).

> "If a man takes care of a leper, his spirit does not become leprous; on the contrary, because of his charity practiced heroically, to the extent of segregating him-

self in the valley of death out of pity for his brother, every stain of sin will be removed from him. Because charity is absolution from sin and the first purification" (p. 760).

Many things will be asked of you that you might think do not pertain to your spiritual progress toward becoming your soul and experiencing God. If you are the sort of person that likes to orchestrate things and decide your own course of action, then having someone around telling you how to live, think, breathe and be will be quite a strain on your ego. But remember, the teacher does not need you and has no need to force his or her position on you. You may come to realize that you need them very much because there is no way you will come to these experiences on your own. The teacher will be more than gracious in allowing you to take whatever breaks from the process of your spiritual development that you may think necessary. But teachers do have the prerogative of teaching you or not teaching you if you are not ready to be a consistent student yet.

> "'I have my sin constantly in mind,' says the psalmist. That keeps their spirits humble. It is a good remembrance when it is joined to hope and trust in Mercy. Half perfections, and even less than half, very often come to a standstill, because they are not spurred by the remorse of having committed grave sins and by

the necessity of making amends in order to proceed towards true perfection. They stagnate like still waters and they are satisfied because they are clear. But even the clearest water will become slimy and foul, unless motion purifies it of the particles of dust and rubble that the wind blows into it" (*The Poem of the Man-God*, Vol. 3, p.537).

What is the process? What needs to be done? What are the problems of soul? When we were first created, we decided to resist some aspects of God and this started all the problems of soul. Our choice in doing things ourselves started a whole cycle of experience that caused a definite drop in the finer spiritual energies existent within our beings. When we decided to indulge our fantasies or desires, the refined energies coming from the God within began to crystallize and densify within us. Our soul is composed of the essence of our experiences. The light coming from the God Self is filtered down with each experience since many of our experiences are less pure than the power of our God Self. When this happens over many lifetimes, our soul has the appearance of mud covering over the bright light of the sun. This densification or encrustation is the experience of our many lives carried on the soul. The various negative emotions that we have indulged, the anger, resentment, hatred, fear, jealousy, lusts of the flesh and other things cause an eclipse of the our divine nature and will be stored in the soul.

The teacher's job is to see the soul of the student and to watch the nuances of your being to see what needs to be cleared off, healed and purged. When the timing is right, the teacher will call up a certain aspect of your nature that needs to be looked at so that you can see it and let it go or have it forgiven. You cannot see these things yourself until the teacher points them out to you. It is annoying sometimes for a teacher to be so in your face and noticing things that you are not able to see. But what are they there for if not to help you? What good would it do for the teacher to know things that you can't know? When they tell you, then you can know them too. It takes some faith and it takes some trust to allow someone to teach you. The soul has many dark and denser qualities in the beginning of spiritual training. Over the lifespan, you have allowed the negation and darkness to just settle into your being as a comfortable, but crotchety old guest in your spiritual house. Many of you are very touchy and super-sensitive when you first start training. Everything is a problem for you. Everything is hard. Anything anyone says to you can cause a huge emotional reaction in you because of your many worries and fears. These are recorded on your soul and must be purged and cleansed for you to become the way God created you and the way your divine nature really is inside.

The teacher waits for the right time to stir your waters and unsettle the mud and impurities resting under the appearance of clarity. These impurities surface and swim in the solution of your life until you can see them. The realization of your blindness causes some remorse and sorrow for having all kinds of residue left over from years and lifetimes of negative experience. Each one is seen and known for what it is and how it got to be there and then you are able to release them into God and be forgiven of them. Jesus and Mary want to take these things from you when you are ready.

The Bhagavad-Gita says, "The Self is the rider in the chariot of the body, the emotions are the horses and the mind the reins." This shows us that we have been living a false pattern of thinking the horse or the reins are our real person. We have made the mistake of thinking that our thoughts were us, that our emotions were us. These are our equipment and our tools, but they are no more us than a pair of shoes. They can be very useful if they are informed of their proper importance and their appropriate job. The Self and soul are the real person inside of you, and every other part of you is a tool for the expression of the real you. Nothing outside of you can fully comprehend or understand your divine nature. Only God can understand God. So the more God you become, the more you will understand soul and Self.
Jesus says in Vol. 5 of *The Poem of the Man-God*:

> "But let the garment of him who is to ascend the throne be purified of all rubbish, so that it may be preserved beautiful for the resurrection, and let his spirit

be purified, so that it may shine on the throne that the Father has prepared for him and he may appear in the dignity befitting a son of such a great king" (p. 847).

"Do love them, so that the Holy Spirit, after the purification, may come to dwell again in those temples that many things made empty and filthy. God, to create man, did not take an angel or choice materials. God took some mud, the most worthless material. Then infusing His breath into it, that is, His love again, He elevated the worthless material to the sublime rank of adoptive son of God" (p. 928).

The problem of soul is that there are so many impurities lodged in your experience that you have to cull them off just like the people who purify metals cull off the impurities when they rise to the top of the fiery caldron. When you find yourself purging emotions or going through changes, it is the impurities that are coming to the surface and the teacher will bring those out of you to purge them away. This is done through communion, confession, or through blessings and healings. It is most definitely done through the word of the priest or teacher. There is nothing that cannot be wiped away if you are repentant and really in need of forgiveness from God. God will fly to your aid when you call. Jesus and Mary will come so quickly when you are really calling them and asking them with heartfelt openness. Just try it sometime and see what happens to you. Do not try to preserve or safe-guard yourself in any way and they will come and make their home with you. Then as you have invited them in, they will start the remodeling of your emotional, mental and spiritual house. They will be the ones who will guide you as to what to keep and what to leave behind. Their love will beckon you into the divine embrace with your soul and Self.

In Vol. 2 of *The Poem of the Man-God,* Jesus says:

> "Always remember: 'I make no difference between you who love me with your spotless purity and you who love me in the sincere contrition of a heart reborn to Grace.' I am the Saviour. Always remember that" (p. 515).

When the impurities are washed away and you have worked out many of your little problems, then the blessing comes of being able to know your soul and Self. Then you will come into divine communion, divine union with the God Self within your own being. You will see the soul and really know yourself. What most people think is that the soul is wonderful and then they don't have to really experience it. If they could see the soul as it is before they do any spiritual work on themselves, they would not be so starry-eyed and dream-struck. They would be a little frightened and horri-fied at the things they have done and said that coated the soul with so much mud and darkness. They would be immediately impressed by how much work they have to do to regain their oneness with God. They would see very clearly that they have fallen quite far from a connection with God and need to do a lot of work to repair the separation that they themselves have chosen. These imperfections and impurities and sins can be cleansed with real spiritual work. If you try to clean yourself up, then you will be going at it the hard way for the simple reason that you cannot see yourself well yet. We need a mirror in order to see ourselves. The teacher or priest is the mirror by which we are able to see ourselves. A priest or teacher is not in this for him or herself. They serve God first and foremost and they are dedicated to aiding their brothers and sisters on the path to oneness with their Creator.

In every life we act and create things that are either reflections of the way God works or they fall far short of the way God acts and is. When we fall short of God's way, a certain density is formed on the soul that becomes a challenge to our spiritual growth. If these accumulate a great deal, they form such a difficult condition that some shock or calamity is necessary to wake us up from our slumber. It is usually a blessing in disguise. In this beneficent grace we are awakened to the possibility of transformation and healing. We are reminded who we are and what is possible for us if we come home to the way God created things. God created us with choice and will. We have definitely exercised it in our own selfish interest. When we get tired of doing things our own way and suffering for it, then we turn to God and God smiles lovingly and compassionately on us as we struggle home. As we come home we are led to one of God's servants who are trained to help us on the way. These selfless servants are conscious of the path of return to God and know the way. They have traveled this way themselves and know the pitfalls and difficulties of such a journey. They are loving and filled with devotion to God and ready and willing to stretch forth their hands to lift you up. They know the pain of living separated from God and they know the trials of coming home. They know that your soul has all sorts of crud on it that will need to be cleansed off, but they hold to the vision of your indwelling divinity. Their love for you will give you hope and faith that it is possible.

So you can leave the books aside, since they mostly do not teach a thing about the soul. The soul, once cleansed, will be so much like God that it will be hard to tell the difference between your personality and that of the Creator. We were made in the spiritual image of God and so we are going to look a lot like God from the soul's perspective and from spiritual sight. Let's let go of the idea that you can describe something and think you can know it that way. Descriptions can come close to pointing you toward an experience, but they are a very stale and pale replacement for a true spiritual experience. Have the courage to say what you don't know and that will put you in the perfect position to open humbly for the real experience of your soul.

God Bless you in your honest striving to know yourself.

Chapter Eleven

Open Up Your Eyes

Can you conceive of a person being healed of an ailment in five minutes? Can a person grow out of a bad habit overnight? If a person has a deep-seated problem that has been there for a long time, can that be changed in a few minutes? Probably you have pondered these questions in your heart and concluded that it is not very likely that people or you will change quickly. Is that not right? In fact, don't you scoff and doubt that a person really has changed when you hear that they have? Isn't it more typical to assume that change is hard and few people have the capacity to make many changes once a condition has persisted in time? This skeptical dynamic and negative expectation is a malaise in our thinking. Who says people cannot change? Who determines what is hard and what is easy? If you want everyone to be like you, then hope for the worst and expect very little in the way of change and progress. The world is full of people who expect to be obstructed in their plans and stifled in their desires. There are few people that do not feel limited and in bondage in relation to something or someone in their life. This is the kind of limitation which stifles most people, and I want to show you and help you to understand it.

There are limitations that God imposes that help you not to presume past a reasonable limit for a created being. These limits are necessary so that pride does not ferment in your mind and heart and cause you to severely separate yourself from God. God may impose a limitation on you that is for your good and stretches you into a deeper consciousness and appreciation for life. Spiritual teachers do the same at times, to help you see something or get straight about something or to overcome something inside you. There are limitations placed on you by the fact that your body doesn't work properly when you are small. In this case, the energy needed to master the body makes you push against those limitations and master the physical world. There are limitations placed on your mind at times when you have to strain against your lack of understanding, to conceive of something more complicated or view a wider horizon. Emotionally, you can be restrained from the more base passions and have to move beyond mere sense gratification and immediate ego satisfaction.

The developmental limitations of childhood are designed to move you into the next phase of your growth and development as an adult human being. They are necessary and uncomfortable and growth producing. When you get old enough to know better and are more on your own, you have to discipline yourself, since you can avoid or resist anyone else's attempts at disciplining you. At this point, limitation takes on a whole new meaning. If you don't pay your bills, either the interest rate might hurt you or the creditors will take back the things you think you own. If you break the law, then you have to pay or actually do jail time. If you are irresponsible in relationships with others, people will avoid you, leave you or mistrust you. Consequences can come fast and hard to those who have been oblivious about the effect their thoughts, words and actions have on other people. A consequence is a limitation imposed on someone; they chose the limitation without necessarily being conscious that they chose it. For example, if you are reckless in traffic but no one has ever told you that you drive like a wild person, when a police officer finally does, there is a penalty to pay. Even if it is just the shock of getting real feedback from people about how you are driving feels to them, that is a consequence of unconscious driving habits.

Let us get back to limitations. If we limit what we can conceive of as possible, we are placing unnecessary and negative limitations on something or someone. What is possible? A blind man being healed? Okay, that's possible because we have heard of Jesus doing that many times. How about healing a blind man who does not have eyeballs in his sockets; is that possible? Well, Jesus did that and made new eyeballs for him and he could see. What about healing a deadly disease where everyone dies? Jesus healed lepers all the time. What about a woman getting pregnant who is too old and does not produce any more eggs? Elizabeth, the mother of John the Baptist, had that experience. What about Lazarus who was dead for four days, rotting and decaying in his tomb, then raised from the dead? Is that possible? From a scientific point of view it is not possible, but with God anything is possible. Jesus demonstrated hundreds of such healings and miracles every day he was here. But even after Jesus ascended, the apostles continued to carry on and perform the same miracles that Jesus did. Saints through the centuries have been so close to God that thousands of the same kinds of miracles, healing and transformations have occurred each year. It is possible at least for some to have these experiences.

Open up your eyes. You have a short memory of the many blessings and healings that you have experienced. Were you not in some emotional pain a while ago and that has lifted or subsided? Did you not have aches or pains in your body and those are mostly gone now and are only a vague memory of something you lived with from the past? If you came to communion daily, you would experience even more blessings. Unwelcome desires and thoughts running through your body, heart, and head will leave you. In a few short months, you will feel the presence of God in your body when you receive a blessing, talk to a priest, or enter into the sacraments.

Change does happen, and there are many experiences that can open your eyes to what is real in life.

We can see our brothers and sisters in our spiritual communities becoming healed. We expect that, since Jesus and Mary want to heal everyone, and each person will receive the healings and blessings they need to move them along. The ones who prevent themselves from growing and moving along are the ones who compare their gifts and their growth with other people and those who secretly wish no one grows past them spiritually. Those two things are the works of darkness and evil. Do you have the sight to see where another person is in relationship with God? Can you tell whether a brother or sister deserves a gift from God? If you cannot discern that, it is because your heart is still hardened with jealousies that others are getting things you feel you should be getting, or you are resentful of anyone else's growth because of how it reflects on you. You have to make a pact with yourself to celebrate everyone's accomplishments and progress. This will keep you humble and make you realize that God's gifts are plenty for you and you are being well taken care of. If you are trying to orchestrate everything yourself, you have already cut God out of the picture due to your anger and pride. Then how can God act in your life if you cannot trust God taking care of you?

Some of you think you are pretty good at seeing what others

need. But when someone receives direct and possibly difficult teaching that may save them from falling on the spiritual path, you worry it might bruise their precious egos. If you
are thinking that what someone else receives would be really
hard for you to receive, you pridefully assume you know that
other person and what they need, and you are saying you
never want to be treated like your parents treated you. If you
are still working on parent issues, you have not really started
the spiritual path yet. I know many people are working on
those issues, and you won't progress very far spiritually if you
keep those hurts and longings and resentments alive in you.
You have to let go of the fact that you were not loved well. It
is a fact and it is a given that all human beings except Mother
Mary and Jesus were not loved well. Get over it soon, would
you? You cannot grow spiritually very much if everything is
about you healing your wounds and pining over lost years. If
you have not asked for forgiveness for all the times you were
mad and acted out, then it stands to reason that you would
not be able to forgive anyone who hurt you. But if you do
not forgive, you will not be released from the karma of those
conclusions. You will pay the uttermost farthing.

When you open your eyes, you see that God is trying to bless
everyone and can move anyone along if they get out of the
way and let it happen. Things don't have to go slowly. When
I look at someone, I see the potential of what their soul can
express. If I held everyone to the limitations that they dem-

onstrate, I would be praying against them and securing them in the place they already are. You are your own worst enemy because you have trouble conceiving what you would be like if you were different, if you were changed. I expect that tonight Jesus or Mary might bless you and lift some of your burdens. I expect that in the morning you will see a whole new way to act, think and feel that will completely change how you are. I expect that you will be different from one time I see you to the next, because I pray for everyone's transformation and growth. It is the dedication of the priests, deacons and teachers to see the God in you and to cultivate that which moves you along spiritually. You cannot do that by yourself, but you can accept the grace and blessings of those whose eyes are opened, so that you can become the way they see you. God sees you perfectly and then prays and blesses you until you manifest that perfection. When you open your eyes, you will know that you are created in the spiritual image of God and that you are an emanation of God's light and a wave in the ocean of God's love.

You can change everything. You can be completely healed, completely alive. You are not limited in any way. Open your eyes and see good coming from everyone you meet and every brother and sister on this planet. Look for the glimmers of light coming from within each person. Be fascinated by that. Listen for the words from God being spoken through the mouths of the children of God. There are a myriad of blessings available to those who love God. You can let go of your anger. You can let go of your pain. The only pain you should welcome is the pain that Jesus and Mary lay on your shoulders to carry out of love for your brothers and sisters. Pain inflicted in any other way is the result of karma and ignorance of your essential nature as gods in flesh. But pain is the way you will emancipate from the condition of your prison of consciousness. If your consciousness is limited, then you are in the suffering which your consciousness creates, and it is not of God. It is self-imposed and resentful. God is waiting for you. Open to God and see what God sees.

Chapter Twelve

You Have Heard It All Before

Just because you can explain something to someone does not mean you have experienced it. If you can say the word "God," it does not mean you know anything about God. Just because you can say the words that you believe in something, does not mean you have had a real experience of the thing you say you believe in. Do you really know God? Do you really know Jesus Christ or Mother Mary? Can you say that you have seen Jesus or Mary or met God face to face? You have to meet someone before you can form a decent opinion of them. If you have anything of an open mind, you would never rely on someone else's opinion of a person you had not met. You would reserve judgment until you met them and talked with them yourself. Wouldn't you apply the same criteria to meeting Jesus, Mary and God?

I hear so many people talking the spiritual teachings who have no idea of what they are talking about. Their words are mostly conjecture and speculation. At best, it is wishful thinking. They are hoping that if they can mouth spiritually sounding words, then they will look like they are having the experience. If a person can talk with flowing emotions about a spiritual topic, it might sound impressive and it might fool some people into thinking they know something. Emotions are no criterion that you know anything in the same way you would from real experience. There are sales people who sell things every day that they only vaguely understand and have no experience with personally. That is the case with the vast smorgasbord of spiritual topics offered to people today. You have to be extremely discriminating to wade through the swamp of offerings out there for spiritual seekers. Most of the stuff out there is exactly that – out there.

Let us become as simple as a little child. When it comes to something spiritual and something real, if it is easy, it is probably not reputable. If it is quick and does not require any personal sacrifices, then it is probably shallow and will not take you very far. If the messengers of those spiritual offerings tell you, by the example of their own messed-up lives, that you can keep your problems and remain as you were, then they have no spiritual integrity. Jesus said, "You must sell all that you have." He meant you cannot keep your old life and your old thinking if you are planning on entering the realm of heaven. He told Nicodemus, "You must be born again." A potential disciple has to go through a rebirth where they are converted to a whole new understanding, a new way of being and most importantly a new mind in

Christ. So something has to die. Something has to give over and be changed in order for you to really, consciously be on the spiritual path.

If you preserve your old life and fear that the spiritual school you are in is jostling your world and scaring you, then you are resistant to changing. You are holding on for dear life to the past. I have to ask you, what is there in your past that is really worth very much? I know it has been full of pain and suffering. The suffering did not help you become one with God; the suffering was caused by choosing the hard road of separation from God. Separation causes all the trouble in life. Union with God will heal your world.

If you have to bargain with a spiritual teacher about the things you want to hold onto and demand that they guarantee you safe passage into the spiritual life without anything dying in you, you are still holding onto your old, miserable life. You might secretly fight with the teacher in your mind and think you have had a marvelous life, a life filled with beautiful experiences, which would make you resistant to change it. What makes you wish for a spiritual life if your former life was so wonderful? You cannot have it both ways. Was it wonderful, or was it painful? If it was painful, then you had help in making it so painful. It was parents or friends that helped make it like that. Later you chose to have it be painful, lonely, sad, scared and worried. The choice for misery and separation cannot be made in the presence of God. The choice of separation cannot be made if you start experiencing a little of God's love inside you.

You've heard everything before. God is within. Let go and let God. Go inside to talk to God. Stop looking at the appearances and judging things by superficial means. Give it all up and let it all go. Spiritual writers tell you to journal things, to meditate, to be silent, to fast on occasion, to still your mind, to enter into communion with God within. All these things you have heard. They are all right in their own way and these things will help you get centered. But how do you do them? Just because you have heard all these things does not mean you have done them. Even if you have done them on your own because you were not able to trust anyone to guide you in these practices, you can't get very far without a teacher.

You need to learn to concentrate your mind and get it disciplined. You cannot pray or meditate well without doing that. You have to develop the devotional muscle and some ability to be spiritually and symbolically, if not actually, on your knees before God. I am not saying to grovel and be servile before God like a dog, but to be completely clear that you were created by God and that you owe everything to the God who created you. You need to learn to pray, to meditate, to bless other people and to become a being filled with light. You have to learn to use the light to see by and the light to guide you through the experiences of your day. You need to learn to not fall into temptation because of anything that might distract you from your relationship to God. Discipline means you have to be vigilant and valiant against evil, never to indulge it even for a minute. You need to pay no attention to it and to look away from anything that might take you into darkness. It is tricky and so you need to be vigilant. It cannot hurt you and it has no power over you whatsoever if you are not interested in it. But it will destroy everything you are trying to build if you let it.

You also need to be interested in being useful to God, because if you are just trying to become spiritual for your own aggrandizement or as some kind of ego trip, then you will not succeed on your journey. You need to trust your teacher and do what they say, or you have no hope of arriving where you want to go. It is only through the work of the teachers and their prayers for you that you are ever going to get where you want to go.

You will gradually have to let go of trying to impress anyone. The only being you should be trying to please is God, and God will not have any lesser gods competing with God. You will need to extinguish within you the desire to get fulfilled through any outside activity, especially through relationships with other flawed human beings. God is in everyone. God is where the people are, but that does not mean that the God in them will be perfectly able to express through that person in loving you. Much experience and history should have taught you that you won't get deep spiritual fulfillment in a personal relationship with another human being because they are still working on a deeper union with God as well. Most people don't have much personal experience of God, so expecting that deep union with a half conscious person is a little ridiculous. They can only channel God's love through them to you if they have some personal experience of God within them. That is rare, so stop trying to get that fulfillment outside you. The realm of God is within you.

Each year, our order grows stronger and gains more integrity and purity. Our ministers and priests grow stronger and more established in their ability to teach and train. We are less likely to indulge darkness in our students. We have asked the priests not to accept a lot of negativity from the students because it shows disrespect for the avenue through which the student is trained. I am not saying that students aren't encouraged to tell their priests what they are feeling and what is going on with them in their counseling sessions. But the master teachers have cautioned the priests not take a lot of negative spewing on the part of the students because it usually comes from someone who is holding onto their negativity and has no intention of letting it go. That is darkness and we will not accept that behavior. This order is about transformation, about light, about truth, and about love. There is no love in accusations. There is no light in spewing negativity and spiteful irritations. Anyone who is putting out words of anger, hatred, resentment or fear is actually indulging the darkness. The darkness is speaking through them. The darkness has a hold on them while they are whining and complaining and saying bad things about someone. We are going to be vigilant about such things. I am not talking about when there is a misunderstanding between two people, because that can be handled by the two of them talking out what they're feeling and what they're experiencing in the interaction. I someone comes at it with accusation, they are always out of balance because they did not stay open enough to find out from the other person what their experience was before forming a judgment about them. That constitutes an unfairness that is essentially wrong because it is acting out of fear instead of love.

Some beginning students will try some of their best intensity and defenses on others in the same style they learned in their family of origin. They might be thinking that if they use their best family skills in the order maybe the order will heal their wounds from their biological family. That is a little silly, because we do not want adults acting like children, so we don't want to act like their parents. We are spiritual parents, not biological parents. You have all gone through that already and we are not in the job of repairing that for you. We will help those wounds, but not by acting out your best model of a good parent. We won't be squeezed into that small box of your DNA training. We are spiritual teachers and we will expect our students to have gone through the growing up years and be self-supporting financially at this juncture. We expect them to be moving into a career that makes enough money to allow them to carry on a spiritual life and spiritual service without a lot of complications. A balanced life is what we are after. A balanced life is where God is placed first, and each individual takes care of themselves financially, economically and emotionally, while following Jesus and Mary on the path back to oneness with God.

All your efforts and sacrifices will be immensely rewarded through the blessing of being close to God. You will be under the loving protection and guidance of Jesus and Mary, and will have all the benefits and joys of such a relationship. In time you will experience the peace that passes understanding.

Chapter Thirteen

Who Is Ready to Be a Student?

S ome people are committed to a life devoted to God. Many people are dedicated and in love with the God that created them, and some are just beginning to know who God is. There are some who may just be exploring what a life devoted to God might look like and how it might feel. Our order is divinely revealed: that means Jesus and Mary want this order, and they want this order to carry out their mission. They define our ways and practices and there is nothing that is not checked out with them before it is set up as a pattern for the members. The mission of our order is to bring souls into the light of Christ and to establish a direct and lovingly close relationship with God. As an order we have the responsibility to bring reality back into the sacraments and to bring integrity to the teacher/student and priest/disciple relationship. Our spiritual exercises and practices are designed to bring students into a personal, experiential awareness of God at the center of their being.

Unless a person has some opening to be taught, they are not called to this spiritual school. They are just paying us a visit and usually a short one. Unless a student has a pretty clear understanding that they don't have all the answers and that they actually need help with some things, then they are probably not drawn to our order at all. So the first thing we as teachers look for in a prospective student is whether they are all set or not, whether they are more interested in letting us know what they know, versus letting us know they need some help with things. If there is nothing the student needs, then they are not going to be open to grow and learn; there is no vacuum inside them for something new and something of God. They are already full of themselves. If the prospective student needs healing from some condition; if they need forgiveness for some error or sin; if they need some teaching in order to really understand how things work; or if they are just in need of guidance to be led into direct union with God; then they are called to our order. But if they don't need healing and don't need guidance and don't need to understand anything because they already know everything and believe they are in as much union with God as they are comfortable with, then they do not become our student. It is just that simple.

We have something to teach, and we want to teach, and we want students who want to learn. We want you to be one of those who want things and want to be trained and taught. Some people act like they have everything down and then months later tell us they have this or that problem. That isn't honest. That is just plain lying about your condition and where you think you are. I have a lot more respect for some-one who says they don't know than for someone who thinks they do when they don't. It is even more blessed to not be sure where you are spiritually than to pretend to know. Hon-esty is very important in students and so is a dose of humil-ity. Humility says I have nothing, I am nothing, anything I am was given to me and everything I become, I will become with God's help. Humility means you are open to being led and guided and taught and you are not trying to pretend you know when you don't. It is genuine and real and hon-est. Humility actually makes it possible to receive something from your teacher because you are in right relationship to the teacher by your receptivity and openness.

If a person does not want anything and does not have an opening to receive anything, our ministers will spend no time with them at all. They will leave them to their fullness, which is merely a selfish fullness, filled with themselves. If a person is open and wants something, then we will work with them and find out what they want or need. This is evi-dent within the first five minutes or so. Our ministers will not waste time imagining that if they explain something just right or coat in just such a way, or present it super well, then a student will get on board. If a student has to be sold the idea of God, then, by nature, they are not looking for God and not really interested. They might think they are doing the ministers a favor by pretending to care. We aren't fooled.

If we have to work really hard to get someone interested in God, then that person doesn't care about God. It is clear and simple.

I want each student in our order to recognize, in time, the mark of someone who is called and is going to be a real student of Jesus and Mary. I want it to be so obvious that without any negative judgment they could say to someone else, "I don't think this is the right path for you," do it dispassionately and with love and not blink an eye. This is absolutely necessary, so that our students are not bought by the flattery of the world or the praise and acclaim of human beings. A servant of God does not receive their reward from human beings, but from God alone. It actually should not matter to you what people think of you, so you should not be thinking about that at all. You should be obedient internally to the divine voice and no other voices. The mark of a real student of Jesus and Mary is their openness to God's will in everything, faithfully and lovingly connected to them with substantial awe for them as perfected beings, and willing to give all in order to serve God and people. The signature of such students will be the light of Christ emanating from their bodies and souls, which will be the regeneration of the flesh body into a body of light. In the early years after Jesus came, perhaps the first 20 or 30 years, students that were baptized actually had a visible change in their countenance that was noticeable to the other disciples. The descent of the Holy

Spirit on the newly baptized made a change in their features that was spiritually noticeable to all who had gone through that experience. In our order, that change is most noticeable when a student comes into the light of Christ where their whole body is filled with light. As Jesus said, "If your eye be single, your whole body will be full of light."

There are only a few orders or spiritual schools that have teachers who are able to bring students into the illumination, and far fewer still who bring people into Self-realization. We want to bring you that experience as soon as you are safely ready. Ready to us means having the humility to not get puffed up about what you are given. Ready to us is that you are not motivated to attain by selfish interests and pride. Ready from our point of view is that you truly put God first in your life and not just temporarily when it is convenient to your sensibilities. Ask your priest how to get ready and what you have yet to do in order to be ready. If you still want to control your own process, where is God in that kind of thinking? How could God surprise you when you are scared of surprises? If you are hell bent on instructing your teachers on the language they need to use in order to reach you, then you are too touchy to be a teachable student at the present time. Maybe you will grow out of the need to impress and make yourself the focus of everything, but maybe not. Then you are more interested in you being god than God being God. Because when God is God, then you are an instrument and a vessel for God and that's it. You don't have your own will. As Jesus said, "I of mine own self can do nothing." "I have not come to do my own will." God's every wish was a command for Jesus and Mary and they were faithful, humble and obedient to whatever God wanted them to do.

Being a disciple is not an easy life. It is the most blessed life there is, but it is not a path strewn with rose petals. There are thorns that come mostly from the people who should know you the best and should have loved you completely. You will learn how to give of yourself and love without thought of return. Coming into union with God will eventually become the whole focus of your life and everything will pale and fade into the background in relationship to that reality.

The priests are taught how to teach and train, so they know what to do and how to do it. You don't have to worry about that. One thing they watch is how our students care about each other. If the priests see someone getting mean and jealous and competitive, even if they think no one knows their inward thoughts, it is noted. We see peoples' thoughts and we can read them like a bad comic book. Often human thought is so degrading and meaningless and selfish that it is embarrassing to call it human. It is really almost completely animalistic. Even animals have more grace and more instinctual integrity than human beings express. They are what they are. Humans are duplicitous and can be so deluded as to not know who they are at all. At least animals act how they are supposed to act and you can predict their behavior. So from the perspective of a true priest, most humans have not graduated to actually being human beings yet. They are still a ways off from that state of being.

This is how we would watch your progress as a student: when you begin to love your sisters and brothers and not concern yourself about what you're going to get, then we can see that the message of Jesus and Mary is starting to happen inside you. It is not just an idea. It is starting to be a practice in your life. Then of course, the next lesson is consistency. Consistency is continuing to do what is right and what works without slacking off and taking small vacations as you adjust to how much you have been giving. If you have to step back and watch your progress, then you are stopping your growth for the weeks or months that you do that. Who is teaching whom? Are you orchestrating how much growth you think you are able to accomplish, or is it okay if your teacher determines what they think you can stretch into and accomplish? Even a worldly school teacher determines when a student should be done with a section of course material and when an exam should be given. If your priest decides you should be done with a certain selfishness or addiction, and you whine and freak and throw a fit to make sure you are still in control, that shows us you are not so sure of your commitment to grow and be taught. We watch all that and see how strong your giving muscle is.

We have had many enthusiastic visitors walk into our seminars and intro classes never to return or continue in training. Sometimes they are not ready. But most of the time they are full of concepts, and want some warmed over retread of spirituality. They want something easy: they do not want a real teacher, or a real relationship with a teacher, or a real relationship with a real God. Their heart is still preserving themselves and fashioning some unique spiritual plan they read about somewhere. They are still a blind person leading themselves around in a dark room bumping into things, and can only imagine what those things are. They read into every situation whatever they want things to be, and thus teach themselves from their own limited vision. They are not ready yet. But sometimes, just sometimes, and rarely, one of these can have their heart broken by the love of a teacher, priest, Jesus or Mary and be opened to something much greater than they have ever conceived before. That is wonderful, but it happens rarely.

I actually have more hope for people who have a strong positive or negative reaction to one of our teachers because it means that it matters to them. Something that occurred between them triggered some important issue from the past which needs to be cleared or healed in order to progress to the next stage of the teaching and spiritual work. If they react and leave in a huff, they were not ready. If they work it through and own their projection onto the teacher, then there is a pretty good chance they will become a full student here in our order.

In *The Poem of the Man-God*, Vol. 2, p. 718, Jesus says:

> "Why, men, do you wish to be fatigued, desolate, tired, disgusted, desperate, when you can be relieved and consoled? Why do you wish, too, My Apostles, to feel fatigue, the difficulty, the severity of your mission, whereas with the reliance of a child you could have cheerful zeal, bright aptitude to accomplish it and realize and perceive that it is severe only for the unrepentant who do not know God, whilst for the believers it is like a mother who supports her child on his way, pointing out to his uncertain steps stones and thorns, nests of snakes and ditches, that he may identify them and thus avoid danger....

> ....But, in the meantime, come to Me you all who are fatigued and tired, you, apostles, and with you all the men who seek God, who weep because of the sorrows of the world, who have become exhausted in their loneliness, and I will restore you. Take My yoke upon you. It is not heavy. It is a support. Embrace

My Doctrine as you would embrace a beloved bride. Imitate your Master who does not confine Himself to bless it, but does what it teaches. Learn from Me who am meek and humble-hearted... You will find rest for your souls, because meekness and humility grant the kingdom both on the earth and in Heaven. I have already told you that the true triumphers among men are those who conquer them by love, and love is always meek and humble. I would never ask you to do things that are beyond your strength, because I love you and I want you with Me in My Kingdom. Take therefore My insignia and My uniform and strive to be like Me as My doctrine teaches. Do not be afraid because My yoke is sweet and its weight is light, whereas the glory that you will enjoy if you are faithful to Me is infinitely powerful. Infinite and eternal...."

Chapter Fourteen

Giving as a Relationship with God

One of the most important things parents can teach their children is how to help their parents. If you are a parent, you need to teach your children how to help clean up after themselves, how to run errands and get things for you, how to dress themselves and hang their towel up. You have to continuously teach your children more complicated things as they grow older because you are standing in for how God teaches all of us – to be an example of how a divine being takes care of us. God does for each human being the same thing a good parent does for their children, only perfectly. God created us with intellect and conscience, the ability to reason things through, and to reflect on whether our actions and thoughts are consistent with the goodness of how we are made. We are endowed with soul and mind. The soul carries the mind of God as well as our experiences within that one mind. Our minds record our experiences and shape the kinds of lessons we need to learn. We are here on earth to learn to become like our spiritual parent, which is God. What did God have in mind for how our true nature should function? What was God's picture of a being that was made in the spiritual image and likeness of God? Who is God and how does God function?

A child grows up to become an adult. A spiritual child is going to grow up to become a spiritual adult. A human being will grow over many lifetimes to resemble God more and more and be a master of creation and the material universe. This goal is inherent in each person as we are all gods in the making. How we learn our lessons and how many difficulties and trials we have to go through depends on us. Most of our troubles arise because we try to do things our own way without the support and help of our Creator. When we wind up in the backwater of our own confused life, suffering the karma of the things we have created, we need to take stock of the fact that we are there because we fell far short of how we were created to be. God saw a perfect plan in creating us, making sure to include within us all the necessary energies that would keep us on track and make us completely resemble God as we grew over time. If we would just try to understand God, at least think about God and try to find out what God is like by forming a relationship with God, then we would discover what God wanted us to learn. There is so much to learn, so many lessons, and so much wisdom to gain that God wants us to have.

Any good parent wants the best for their children. Any good child wants to learn all they can from their parents in order to please them. That is natural and normal and works well if parents would take on the job with some sense of connection to God and some love for other people. A good child will try to please their parents and do everything they can to learn and grow and help in every way they can. Much of the learning that children do is by way of imitating the things parents do. It is the same with a relationship with God, Jesus and Mary. Jesus and Mary are the prototype parents for everyone on earth. Jesus and Mary are the ones who are responsible for the growth of all human beings living on this planet. God decided that they were the ones and even though there are and have been many avatars and wise ones sent to earth to teach and help people, God selected Jesus and Mary to be the sovereigns of Earth. The other teachers that are here or were here are still blessed by God and were sent by God to teach and help people, but out of all these, God selected our Master and Mother to be the ones who are ultimately responsible for the souls of human beings coming to earth. The evolution of humans is under their direct training and love. God decided that. We did not decide that. You can ask God directly if you get quiet enough and God will tell you. You may not be called to this particular path, but whatever path you are really called to, one day you will find that above whoever you are working with, there stand Jesus and Mary as the most honored and most blessed of all the human beings who have ever walked the earth. It is not bias that causes me to say this. It is not familiarity with Western ways that makes me say this. It is an experience of them as beings that shows me who they are in relationship to God and the earth. You can find this out for yourself if you ask God whether this is true. To put it more simply, if you ask Jesus and Mary to come and be with you, you will begin to know who they are.

The teaching from God is that parents are supposed to be patterned after God. God is the ultimate and perfect teacher. Through God's love we are introduced to perfect love. In a relationship with God, you will become familiar with who God is and how God functions and teaches. God will inspire you to move closer to God and be more like God. God gives to you everything you ask for and will continue to care and bless you if you only wish. God is consistent and gives completely unconditional love, guidance and help for you. You can see that parents are not so perfect, not so unconditional and hardly consistent in their teaching, love or training of their children as God is.

So each of you has to make the best of life and learn the things you were not taught when you become adults. In an ideal world, you would find other adults to model your behavior after and follow their directions. You would have to fill in the gaps with your own experience and self-discipline in order to become the kind of person that God had in mind when God created you. As you start to understand how God gives you everything and cares for you, you begin to realize that you need to learn to do the same with other people. This is a great awakening when you see that you are created to shine, to radiate light, to give and to love like God.

To get to this point of this awakening, our spiritual training recreates an ideal environment for your growth. At first, you are receiving and taking love from those around you. You soak up the love and bask in the protection of those who are stronger than you. This is a temporary condition of training and discipline, and in many ways you are being given the gift of enjoying the protection of the stronger ones on the earth. Teachers hold under their protection many people who have not yet learned to participate in life as a help to other people. They are still learning and soaking up love and it has not yet dawned on them to be able to give or help in any way. It is natural for spiritual children to receive and learn and grow, but it is also natural for children to want to give of themselves by modeling after those who are stronger and further along on the path of self-mastery. There is no need for pride or selfishness in the process if you are humble and starting to know your Creator.

If you observe the people who serve, you will notice that they spiritually shine more than the ones who are served. That is the way Jesus and Mary taught us and that is the way this order is built and established. The ones who serve are always the ones who have learned to love more than those who receive. They have sacrificed their lives for a greater good which is the bringing in of souls into the presence and light of God. Nothing brings us more joy and no action can bring a more profound depth of love and growth of soul than serving God through serving our brother and sister souls on the earth. The giving muscle starts as a weak strand, giving in fits and starts. The fledgling giver is a new disciple without much experience in loving others, who starts to use the powerful muscle of love in short and hesitant stages as that muscle develops. At first they are like new children, just drinking deeply of the food offered to them and enjoying the love of those who are caring for them. If they come in all wounded and strange, their suspicions and defensiveness take a little while to soften and relax. As they let their sisters, brothers and teachers love them, they grow in leaps and bounds towards the light. They emulate and follow the example of their stronger sisters and brothers who have long since adjusted to a life of giving and loving other divine beings like themselves. You may think that your older brothers and sisters on the path are a lot older, but they have only been around a little longer than you in most cases. Some of the more seasoned priests may have been serving for years and are solid and reliable fountains of love and grace that you may take advantage of. You can come to them with your needs and they will not turn you away. They will give you what you need – not necessarily what you want. Because sometimes what you want are the bad habits in you screaming from the desolation of the past and demanding attention. Those bad habits are gnarly and desperate and usually brook no opposition to their desires. The discipline of a deacon or a priest might seem firm and tough, but it is the closest thing to real love that you might have received in this life so far. The example of Jesus and Mary becomes the prototype and model for all true and holy love. As Jesus said, "I did not come to be served but to serve." That is our example. Jesus came to love, not to receive love.

Our goal for each person that comes to be trained with us in the Order of Christ/Sophia is to become Self-reliant on God and a channel of grace, love and light for everyone they meet. Whether people receive you that way is irrelevant from our point of view. But your capacity to love, as well as your patience and understanding, is vital if you are going to be a successful disciple of Jesus and Mary. Giving of yourself is the calling card of the true disciple. Acting promptly with enthusiasm and an open heart is the way to carry yourself throughout your day. Moving your body slowly with great difficulty and sluggishness may happen as a lifelong pattern of resistance and resentment acting out as selfishness. Love moves swiftly, not slowly. Letting go of your past and acting like a divine son or daughter of God will take care of all your problems. Your fears will evaporate as you come into accord with the patterns and practice of the order. Your pride and fear will show up in your interactions with your older brothers and sisters and you will have to let those go. Your biological age will become irrelevant as you see that many disciples much younger than you have gone much farther in their relationship with God than you have as yet. Life experience helps, but your love and relationship with God is more important to us.

The final thing I want to talk about in the life of a disciple of Jesus and Mary is your ability to give of yourself, not just for a short time, but for the rest of your existence. I know it would seem to some of you who are experiencing this spiritual path for the first time that you are in no position to commit to this process until you know much more. That is reasonable, it does take time and you are not asked to commit more than you know at any point on the path. In fact, it is a surprise to some of you that you have to ask us formally to teach you before you get an actual teacher assigned to you. A deacon or priest will teach you in the beginning stages as you get your feet wet and learn the patterns that will set you free of the chains that bind you. Later you might have one of the Master Teachers teaching you. But for now, many of you will be assigned a minister to teach you if that is your desire. That can only happen if you know that you would be willing to actually do what the teacher says and be in direct and responsive communication with your teacher. But I want you to consider that giving of yourself also includes signing on for a long, long time to serve God, Jesus and Mary. It is not just until retirement. There is no retirement from being a son or daughter of God. There is no tired-ness that would justify coasting into death of the physical body. As the physical body is only a very small part of who you are, it would be a misconception to imagine that your body would be telling you what to do at any point in your discipleship to Jesus and Mary. Your body is a vehicle for the light of Christ and it is to have no leading say in what your soul wants you to do. Over time, as you become more soul and less outer consciousness, your soul will be the motivat-ing power of your dedication and service. Your soul will be more and more obedient and humble to God. Your soul will remember the love of your Creator who built you and you will learn that God has complete rights over you. You will be faithful to that relationship above all else, above family con-siderations, above allegiances to parents or children, above loyalties to job or relatives, above any other loyalty. God is the only one we serve.

But can you give for the duration of your existence as a soul without looking for a break from giving? Can you give as much as the early disciples who picked up and left their fam-ilies, their careers, their homes and relatives and walked into the future with Jesus and Mary? They had found something so powerful, so real, so loving and so eternal that none of their earthly, temporary considerations were meaningful by comparison. That is giving everything and following Jesus and Mary as disciples of the Christ. You are being invited into that relationship through our work here. We have done that. Can you? Will you give of yourself the same as we have? That is offered to you as a gift to your soul.

Chapter Fifteen

What Does It Mean to Be a Disciple?

Disciple sounds a lot like discipline, doesn't it? The word "disciple" actually comes from the Latin word, "discere" meaning "to learn." A disciple is one who accepts and embraces a particular teaching or training. The disciples of Jesus learned his teachings and accepted his training. Discipline means training. You could not expect to learn carpentry if someone did not show you how to do it. You would apprentice to someone who was a master carpenter in order to learn the many things that they know about working with wood and construction. In the same way, if you wanted to learn about God and your own divinity, you would have to apprentice with one who knows about those things and has a complete knowledge and experience of God. Jesus was one who was completely one with God. He also had the audacity to proclaim that oneness, which is why he was hated by the religious leaders of the time. Either you would have to be crazy to say such a thing, or it was true that Jesus was one with God.

A disciple undertakes a certain discipline that produces a

particular result. Jesus said, "A disciple is not above the master. It is enough that the disciple be like the master." In other words, it is important when undergoing training that you become like your teacher and begin to practice the same actions and consciousness that your master does. This entails following the example of the one showing you how to function, how to be, how to think, and how to behave. Jesus trained his disciples in everything having to do with life. He trained their thinking, their words, their expressions, their body movements, their feelings, their allegiances and their relationships. There was no part of the disciple's existence that did not come under the loving, watchful guidance of Jesus. All Master Teachers function the same way in guiding and training their disciples. There is no other way to come into a full and complete experience of God without entering into this relationship. The religions have lost that one-on-one connection whereby a teacher enables the student to grow in consciousness and let go of everything in themselves that is not God. The only way for a student to be truly themselves is to come under training with one who knows God and has the authority to impart that experience to a disciple.

A teacher is not self-appointed as if they came up with the idea themselves that they wanted to teach people things and would call themselves "teacher." That is not the way things happen in the spiritual life. Teachers are ordained and commissioned to teach by their teacher. They are trained and empowered to follow in the footsteps of the one who trained them. They are doing very well if they teach with the same consciousness and love as the one who trained them. The "would-be" teachers, who have a great idea one day and pronounce themselves teachers, are wolves in sheep's clothing and you should definitely run far away from them. Unless a person has accepted training under a God-realized Master Teacher, they have no right to teach anyone. When you place yourself in surrender to someone who is blessed with the rights to teach you, you will be taken on angel's wings to the interior heaven where God resides. You will be tested and tried to make sure your dedication is strong and your love for God is real. You will be supported in your ascent out of the mud of your previous existence, and all of your former life will seem dead and old to you as you move along the spiritual path. No part of your life, thoughts or feelings will be hidden from the scrutiny of the teacher. You are an open book on all levels to a real teacher and they will patiently and lovingly guide you to a real relationship with God.

The disciple is asked to do things that are sometimes difficult or scary. There are resistances and troubles any disciple has acquired from early life that need definite transformation and regeneration. Each of these areas of difficulty and trouble is meticulously worked through under the direction of the teacher to be free of all the blocks to being one with God. Sometimes it might be very hard for you to take the loving scrutiny and intense gaze of the teacher. Other times, the teacher's love for you will melt your heart, and other relationships will seem pale compared to how pure and complete that love is. How much can you stand to be loved? How much love can you stand before you get uncomfortable and want to rush out and get a break from it? The teacher watches everything and feels your energy and waits until the time is right for each new lesson and instruction. Every part of the disciple is grist for the mill that will turn you into usable bread to feed other disciples who come after you. You are as grains of wheat in the hands of the great bread maker. Your grain must be winnowed and threshed in order to separate out the good part of the grain from the chaff. Then the grinding and breaking occurs where your outer sense of yourself is broken and crushed by the loving hands of one who knows what you will turn into before you do. When you lovingly submit to this grinding, you are ground into whiteness and then water and yeast is added to your grain. This is the yeast of love and grace that quickens your matter. The water is the understanding and patience of the teacher. Then you are kneaded until you are pliable and you are allowed to raise up again. You are encouraged and praised for your striving and your efforts at discipline. You are then kneaded again and pressed down to make sure the whole of you is fully accepting of the grace and love that will change you and raise you up. In the final rising, you are becoming more who you will really be when you are served as food for hungry souls. But the process is not complete until the fire of transformation completes the process of making you congeal into a finished product to serve to others. Then you are who you were created to be and will feed many future disciples on the energy and consciousness of your own being.

In *The Poem of the Man-God*, Vol.1, p. 351, Jesus said, "The first condition of a disciple is to obey his Master, knowing that the Master knows, and can give but just orders." In Vol. 2, Jesus continues: "Absolute respect, to be able to speak, to be silent, to ponder, to act, are the virtues of the true disciple in order to make proselytes and serve God" (p. 180), and also on p. 659, "Disciples are not above their Master but they can do what the Master does, when they do it for a holy reason."

You are not a disciple unless you are under the direction of someone who can guide you. It is in your acceptance and dedication to do what the teacher guides you to do that you will attain the balance and connection to God that you seek. If you do not follow and you spend much of your time look-ing away, you will miss the lessons that are so necessary to your growth. If you remain fixed on the teacher and pay at-tention to every word, every nuance of action, every energy that comes from the teacher, you will gradually and success-fully gain the poise and balance that only the God Self un-derstands. You will become like the teacher. You will not be them and it has nothing to do with imitating someone. You are you and the teacher is the teacher. Do not try to pattern your expressions and your personality on the teacher. Just be yourself, but pay close attention to the whole life of the teacher, not just what they say because then you will learn what it takes to be one with God.

You would not follow someone unless you suspect that where that person is, is where you want to go. You would only follow if you sense that they have some knowledge or experience you want to have. You would have to be honest about where you are, what you know, and how far you seem to be from where the teacher is. The circumstances of your life would have to give you some pause to consider that you are not where you want to be. You would feel longing to be somewhere else with a different mind and a different consciousness. When you see someone who apparently knows where they are going, you would have to keep close track of them and persevere in order to know what they know. It would not be easy because the experiences and work that the teacher has already attained would take some time. Persistence and dedication would be vitally necessary or you would not get all of the lessons you would need to arrive at the place of connection to the God Self within.
Jesus says:

"To follow Me as a disciple means renouncing all affections for one only love: Mine. The selfish love for oneself, the guilty love for riches, sensuality or power, the honest love for one's wife, the holy love for one's father and mother, the deep love for and of children and brothers, must all yield to My love, if one wishes to be Mine. I tell you solemnly that My disciples must be freer than birds flying in the sky, more free than winds blowing across the firmament without anyone or anything holding them back. They must be free, with no heavy chains, with no ties of material love, without even the thin cobwebs of the slightest barrier. The spirit is a delicate butterfly enclosed in the heavy cocoon of the flesh and even the iridescent impalpable web of a spider can slow down its flight or stop it all together: the spider of sensuality, of the lack of generosity in sacrifice. I want everything, unreservedly. The spirit needs such freedom and generosity in giving, to be sure that it is not entangled in the cobwebs of affections, habits, considerations, fears, stretched out like as many threads by the monstrous spider which is Satan, the robber of souls.

If one wants to come to me and does not hate in a holy manner, father, mother, wife, children, brothers and sisters, and one's very life, one cannot be My disciple. I said: 'hate in a holy manner....' I say that you must hate the heaviness of love, the sensual passionateness of love for your father and mother, wife and children, brothers and sisters, and for your very life, on the contrary I order you to love your relatives and life with the light freedom of spirits. Love them in God and for God, never postponing God to them, endeavoring and taking care to lead them where the disciple has already arrived, that is to God, the Truth. You will thus love God and relatives in a holy manner, safeguarding each love, so that family ties will not be a burden but wings, not a fault, but justice. You must be prepared to hate even your lives in order to follow Me. He hates his life who without fear of losing it or making it sad from a human point of view, uses it to serve me. But it is only the appearance of hatred....

....Because to be my disciples implies going against the stormy and violent trend of the world, of flesh and of Satan. And if you feel that you do not have the courage to renounce everything for My sake, do not come to me, because you cannot be my disciples" (*The Poem of the Man-God*, Vol. 3, p. 34).

If the world still holds many alluring and interesting things for you, perhaps you are not ready for the spiritual path. You may feel that your life has been so painful up to this point that it is about time that you have some joy and excitement for a change. That is the frustration that you feel because of having to suffer at the hands of care-givers and grow through all of that. Well, cheer up. There is no person alive who has perfect parents, perfect in patience or in love. All have suffered and fallen short of the experience of being one with God. That should be sufficient motivation to cause you to want the experience of God's love since it is perfect and not subject to emotions and fickle passions. God's love is the benefit for being a true disciple. Let the amusements and desires of the world slip away and you will awaken to the joys of experiencing life and God's creation from an entirely Godly perspective. You will come to experience the true meaning of life which is to let God express through you. Then you will come to know how God wants to experience the beauty of creation and the vital powers of human beings as they love, serve, create and imagine.

The disciple has a responsibility to follow because of their commitment to be trained and taught. The teacher will take you as far as you want to go. But the teacher lives under a different level of responsibility: to teach is to stand at a place that is higher up than where the student stands. Otherwise, how could the teacher raise you up unless they were at a higher level of vibration than you? The cost of discipleship is your life, simply because the life you have and the person you think you are will all be changed. You may have a common fear of change for the simple reason that you are not sure you will recognize yourself if you make too many transformative changes. But it is necessary to trust the process and allow yourself to be reformed and reborn in the image of God, just as you were created when you were first conceived in God's mind. The cost is your life. But was it ever your life? Do you have, or have you ever had, a separate life apart from God? No. Your life has always been borrowed from the one energy of God. You thought it was separate and personal because your parents wanted you to be an individual instead of a daughter or son of God like you were built to be. The cost is your mind. But has it ever been your personal mind? No. The thoughts that you have are simply the use you make of the one mind out of which all thought expresses. It is true that as you progress on the spiritual path your thoughts become more pure and powerful for the simple reason that you are thinking more clearly the way God thinks and not the way animal humanity thinks. There is only one mind and that is God's mind.

This is a story from Jesus' life taken from *The Poem of the Man-God*, Vol. 2, p. 417:

> (...and Jesus picks a fully ripe dandelion growing among the stones. He raises it gently to His mouth, blows and the dandelion dissolves into tiny umbrellas, which wander in the air with their little tufts on top of the tiny handles.) "See? Look... How many have fallen on My lap as if they were in love with Me? Count them... They are twenty-three. They were

at least three times as many. And the others? Look. Some are still wandering, some have fallen because of their weight, some, which are proud of their silvery plume, are haughtily rising higher, some are falling into the mud that we made with our flasks. Only… Look, look… Of the twenty-three that were on My lap, seven more have gone. That hornet flying by was enough to blow them away! What were they afraid of? Or by what were they allured? Were they afraid of its sting? Or were they allured by its beautiful black and gold hues, or by its graceful appearance, its iridescent wings?… They have gone… Following a deceitful beauty. Simon, the same will happen to My disciples. Some will go because of their restlessness, some because of their inconstancy, their pride, their dullness, their frivolity, their lust for filth, some for fear, some because of their foolishness. Do you think that in the crucial hour of My mission I shall have beside me all those who now say to Me: "I will come with you?" The tiny tufts of the dandelion, which the Father created, were more than seventy… and now there are only seven left on My lap, because some more have blown away by this puff of wind that has caused the thinner stems to flutter away… It will be like that. And I am thinking of how much you have to struggle to be loyal to me…."

It is painful to watch our brothers and sisters fall into doubt and struggle to remain faithful to the spiritual process of discipleship. But Jesus had many of his disciples leave after he told them that they had no life in them unless they ate his flesh and drank his blood. Since most of the people were dense and stupid, they thought this saying was literal and were offended, and thousands left Jesus. He was talking about communion, but he was also talking about his flesh and blood being the most pure and powerful substance we could possibly take into ourselves. His gift to us was the complete purity of his being through the communion.

There are a number of reasons why people leave our order and the spiritual path. Usually it is because things get hard and the attachments to your former patterns and addictions start fighting you and causing many stormy doubts to fly up into your mind. If you indulge them, they get stronger. Also, there will be people who propose a much easier path to you or a much easier life. If you listen and fall for this temptation, you will lose your way and not be faithful to what Jesus and Mary are calling us to do. Jesus said, "No greater love has a person than to lay down your life for your friend." This is the high water mark of love among Jesus' disciples.

Put your whole heart into your discipleship, into your training so that you can answer the Master's question of "What have you brought me?" Your answer can then be, "I have done everything you asked me to do. I have given myself completely in your service and I kneel before you empty of myself and waiting your judgment and blessing. I hold nothing back from you, I give my all in service to you. I ask nothing for myself except to be made acceptable in your sight. Here I am Master, without one plea. Use me, as I am yours. Thank you."

Chapter Sixteen

Master Jesus: God's Greatest Gift

Many years have passed since Jesus spoke his words to the apostles. We think sometimes that since it was so long ago that his teachings don't apply to us in our present day. Maybe the times have changed and there should be a whole new approach to the spiritual path and to service to God. Actually, nothing has changed. We have not advanced that much since Jesus and Mary walked on earth in flesh bodies. The fact is that Jesus and Mary are closer and more accessible now than ever. They are living in our world and we are encompassed on every side by their power, their presence and their love. There is nothing we can do about it, since we were not consulted about what their job would be. The gift they bring us is so much more vital and available that we merely have to reach up in thought to who they are and we get an immediate lift in consciousness. As Jesus said, "I am closer than hands and feet."

In our present time, many people still think of Jesus as a historical figure that does not have any real bearing on our present life. They revere him as a decent, loving man who angered the Jews and prophesied some things and disturbed others a great deal. He drew a small band of followers from some of the more backward towns around Jerusalem and cured a fair number of ill, blind and lame people. He raised a few people from the dead, but that is as far as it goes for most people. Many do not see him, and don't know him as alive and real in the here and now, as we speak and see.

I want you to know that you can meet him and talk to him, and he will definitely be interested in what you have to say. He is not distant in some moment of historical time. He is closer than your breath. He is waiting so patiently for you to invite him to be near you to teach you. He wants to take your sins and burn them in the great fire so you won't be burdened by them anymore. He wants to take you in his arms and hold you to protect you from the darkness and evil of the world. He has the power to heal you, he has the power to save you from yourself and the temptations that suffocate and trouble you. Nothing is impossible to him because he paid the price of his total sacrifice and surrender to the will of God by his crucifixion and death on the cross. He became victorious over death, resurrected and ascended to the highest heaven as the first son to return to the Creator in a purified and illuminated state. If you want to know him, you merely have to ask. He will respond. I promise that if your desire is sincere, he will fly towards you with great anticipation of accepting you. He wants nothing more than to free you from the burdens of your former life and take you to himself so you too, can be one with your Father-Mother God.

What is stopping you from letting go of your troubles and your problems? Do you want to keep them? Haven't they been weighing you down and stifling your heart with fears and worries? Are those problems so comfortable and familiar to you that you wouldn't trade them for a life of hope and joy? What would it take for you to give them up? Jesus said, "Come to me all you who labor and are heavy laden and I will give rest to your souls." That is an amazing promise. We will be unburdened if we merely come and lay our faults, our sins, our problems, our fears, our worries, our longings and resentments at his feet and he will heal our whole being. I know this is true because it happened to me. If it can happen for me, it can happen for anyone.

When your fears, worries, problems and sins are lifted, forgiven and burned away, you will be starting on the road of being useful to God. Jesus and Mary will fill your every need. They will hold you in their embrace and give you light to see. They will pour wisdom into you that will surpass anything the world knows. In this embrace you will be healed of the past pain and hurt. You will start to get a sense of what you are doing here and who you are as a created soul/

Self in creation. Your healing will be so profound and your growth so swift that you will not be able to control the process. You will soon accept that God knows what should be done and you will start to trust God's intelligence. You will start receiving interior guidance from the divine part of you. The God Self will show you how to act and what to say. In this process, your heart will fill with love for your sisters and brothers and you will want to know how to help them. You will feel their sufferings and will be asking God how to help those people with whom you come in contact.

At this point, you need to learn the tools of really being able to serve God and aide in the work of drawing souls to Christ. In the Order of Christ Sophia, you will train with a priest or teacher in the art of teaching and counseling. When you observe souls, do not overlook anyone. Watch for the fire in the eyes and light in the touch of people who are searching for God. Become a watcher of souls, looking for the hungry ones, those who are seeking real food. Be willing to give spiritual food to those who are hungry. Be eternally ready to heal those who long for healing, those who long to be freed from the wounds of their own illness, either in mind or body. Do not hesitate to take from people the ugly, dark things and sins that they are suffering from, so that they can be cleansed and healed. Do not disdain anyone who sincerely seeks healing or desires to be taught the ancient teachings. Give these teachings to those who pay the price. That price is humility and integrity. Look for sincere souls and those who have been wounded by life or by their own hand. Many of the problems you hear about are not that complicated, but they are as individual as the grains of sand on the shore. Each fish has its own type of scales different from every other fish in the sea. You need to be able to identify the various types so that you approach them with the right bait and the right patience.

You will learn to be a true fisher of human beings. You will be given the sight to see the problems and the ability to speak the truth without holding back when it is time to speak. You need to learn the art of dropping the bait into the waters and letting it attract people. Your bait may be a kind word, an unusual way of looking at something, a glance that understands, a helping hand or practically anything that brings you into rapport with another person. The simpler your responses to people, the better. People who are new to the path are understandably skittish about being fooled, manipulated and hurt. Most people have been abused or mistreated in some way and are naturally and understand-ably vigilant when it comes to abuses of power. The power of God will be strong in you, so you will have to moderate the fire so that it doesn't ignite someone too soon. Remember, God said God was a consuming fire. The purity of love that has grown in you took a long time to develop and you must not assume that people will just be able to come up to speed with that intensity on first meeting you. When they meet you, they will either be drawn or repelled. Some will have both of these competing experiences about you at the same time. The more resistance they experience, the more they are truly called. But their life at present has so many entangling attachments that there will be a tearing occurring before they are able to extricate themselves from the ties that bind them. Their families, their relationships, and their previous conclusions about spirituality will all come up for review and they will struggle like a fish on a hook.

Once a person is on the hook, you have to pay close attention to them and not let them out of your consciousness. This means you have to touch into to them in visualization and prayer and stoke the fire of the presence of God in blessing them and holding them in the embrace of Jesus and Mary. This way, they will be able to make their own decision without fighting you. Most people are terrified of life and hurt by many conditions of living. They sometimes struggle when someone loving comes along to care about and embrace them. They cannot believe that love or comfort is possible for them, and so will resist it. That is normal, so don't be deceived by what they are saying or doing. They will toss and turn and may be angry or reactive, but don't pay any attention to the content of their comments. When they struggle hard, let loose the line and they will feel free in their choice. When they let go a little, draw them in like reeling in the line. When the hook is firmly planted in them, they might struggle, but they are coming home and will gradually feel loved and comforted as they draw near the boat, the body of Christ. You know they will be much more fulfilled and whole if they get in that boat. They will become peaceful and still. They will gradually know that they are loved and will submit to the process of the becoming food for others in the body of Christ.

When vacationing, I observed the pelicans on the ocean fishing in the morning. They would fly flapping their wings only a few times, sailing over the water, their keen eyes watching every glisten of the reflections of the fish in the sunlight. Then they would just free fall with half stretched wings into the sea and grab the fish in their beaks. Sometimes they wouldn't get anything. But more often than not they would, and it would be quick and painless. Gulped down in a moment, the fish becomes a part of their body and they swoop away for another one. They were focused, vigilant, unfailing in their task. I had to admire their persistence and skill. They rested at times just floating on the water bobbing up and down with the waves. So, too, when you become a fisher of human beings, you will have to be vigilant and watchful, with keen observation skills, scanning the horizon for souls who are waking up. When you see them, you will want to drop near and say something or do something that may encourage them. You have to fan the flame of that deep longing in their soul for God. If you are diligent and determined, nothing will be impossible for you because you are working for God and Jesus Christ and Mother Mary. There will be times of rest when you are able to sit and meditate on your days catch and perhaps digest and assimilate what you have experienced.

How can you be a fisher of other people if you are still worried about yourself and your own life? If you feel God's love well up inside of you and you know it's there, you will not lack for anything. You will be confident that God is taking care of you and your needs are covered. You will trust that Jesus and Mary's love is sufficient for you and that God will take care of everything if you just keep working in the harvest, bringing in those fish that will make good food for others. If you have been loved so much, why? way you can to God? What wouldn't you want to give back in the most wholesome price, would you be willing to pay for the gift of oneness with God?

The apostles and those who followed them have angled for people's souls to save them. Patiently, subtly, impatiently and brashly, they have set their nets and fished. The bishop of the church wears a miter, a headgear shaped like the head of a fish with the mouth slightly open. At casual glance it looks like a symbol of the pomp of office, topping off his rich vestments. But there is more to the story because the bishop is showing himself as the fish itself, the one caught by Jesus. He is inwardly humbling himself and yet must turn and fish for others. The open place is a symbol of the crown chakra, open to the power from above.

Jesus came at the beginning of the Piscean Age, the sign of the fishes. A favorite symbol of the Christian church is the Greek word for fish "I, Ch, Th, Y, S" being spelled using the initials for Jesus Christ, God's son and savior. Jesus was able to live in the abyss of this mortal life as one in the depths of waters, without sin. Some have said that the sea symbolizes the spiritual realm, and the boat the soul body in which we function in that realm. All life has its origin in water, so ancient philosophers chose the fish as a symbol of the life germ. Fish are prolific and human sperm resemble them. Fish are a symbol of the hidden mysteries of truth, gained by initiation. Casting the nets on the right side of the boat is the right or positive way to form the union of the two currents in head and heart that brings about the transformed mind and sacred heart of Jesus. During the Piscean Age, the fish was the sign of divinity, as was the lamb previously, and the ox before that. The human being is the symbol of the divine in the Aquarian Age.

In some cultures, fish were sacred to Venus and are still being eaten on Venus' day, which is Friday. The Hebrew word NUN means both fish and growth. The Jews were led to victory by the son of Nun (fish), who was both Joshua and Jesus. Even to this day women vowed to devotion to God and celibacy are called Nuns since they are the "fish" caught by Jesus in the net of a disciple somewhere. Among early Christians, three fishes were used to symbolize the trinity. The early Christians also likened converts to fish who cannot live except through the waters of baptism. The whale that swallowed Jonah represented initiation into the mysteries, the great fish representing the darkness of ignorance that engulfs us when we are thrown over the side of the ship to be born into the sea of life.

Fish have often been associated with world saviors: Vishnu, the Hindu redeemer was expelled from the mouth of a fish as his first incarnation. Oannes, the Chaldean savior, appeared in the costume of a fish with the head and feet of a man protruding below the fish body. He taught the people all that they needed to know including how to construct cities, build temples and compile laws. He gave them insight into letters, arts and geometry. He ate nothing, but when the sun set, he retired again into the sea and passed the night in the deep, for he was amphibious.

There are legends that long before human beings, there existed a species of composite creatures that were destroyed by the gods. According to records taken from some of the temples, the human race evolved from an amphibious crea-

ture. Primitive human beings may have had gills and were
partly covered with scales. The human embryo demonstrates
the possibility of such a state. We originated in water and so
early writers saw fish as the progenitors of human beings.
The gall of a fish was used to restore sight to Tobias' father in
the Apocrypha account. Fish were also depicted on certain
Chinese coins as an emblem of good fortune. The fish is a
psychic being of penetrative motion, related to the subconscious. Because of its bobbin-like shape, it is sometimes seen
as a kind of "bird" of the nether regions. The practice of fishing amounts to extracting the elusive treasure called wisdom
from the subconscious elements of deep-lying sources. To
fish for souls also implies fishing in the soul. The one fishing
is able to work upon the very sources of life.

> Simon Peter said to them, "I am going fishing." They
> said to him, "We will go with you." They went out
> and got into the boat, but that night they caught
> nothing. Just after daybreak, Jesus stood on the shore,
> but the disciples did not know that it was Jesus. Je-
> sus said to them, "Friends, have you any fish?" They
> answered, "No." Jesus said to them, "Cast the net to
> the right side of the boat, and you will find some." So
> they cast it, and now they were not able to haul it in
> because there were so many fish. The disciple whom
> Jesus loved said to Peter, "It is the Lord!" When Si-
> mon Peter heard that it was the Lord, he put on some

clothes, for he was naked, and jumped into the sea. But the other disciples came in the boat, dragging the net full of fish, for they were only a few hundred yards from land (John 21:3).

Chapter Seventeen

Holy Communion

In every one of our Centers of Light, we have communion first thing in the morning. We meditate for one half hour beforehand to do our spiritual exercises or to prepare ourselves for receiving the body and blood of Jesus. If you have had a real communion, then you know how beautiful that experience is. You would have felt a contact and a love from Jesus and Mary that is profound and simple, while being intense and overwhelming at times. Each time you partake of the body and blood, it tastes a little different, even though it is always the same unleavened bread and the same grape wine. The body contains the consciousness and mind of Jesus, while the blood contains the experience and spirit of Jesus. Each time you receive communion with an open heart, you are changed a little by the love and forgiveness of Jesus and Mother Mary. She is in the sacrament of communion as well because she was the vessel for the Christ. She was the first chalice for the pure energies of the Christ when God gave Jesus to the people of the earth in payment for all the sins humanity covered the earth with over the centuries.

The sacrament of communion is the only sacrament that can be repeated each day, while the other sacraments can only be done once, with the exception of the sacrament of confession. Communion is the daily staple of our spiritual food. It is the flesh of a God given daily for the atonement of our souls with the Creator. Through communion we regain our son/daughtership and we are gradually brought back into the perfection of how we were created. Jesus instituted this sacrament as the greatest gift anyone has ever brought to humanity. Communion is the way back into union with God. Jesus said, "Except you eat the flesh of the Son of Man and drink his blood, you have no life in you." Jesus emphatically states that life is experienced through receiving his flesh and blood. We take this statement literally and that is why we celebrate communion every morning. We really do transform the literal bread and wine into the real flesh and blood of Jesus Christ to feed the faithful disciples.

I know in the Christian churches, they have communion and it is primarily a commemoration, like a ceremony that has no real power or authority in it. They are going through the motions and do not have the authority to change the bread into the body and the wine into the blood of Jesus. Only one who is anointed and ordained with the authority of the word and the real priesthood has the authority to transmute the bread and wine into the body and blood of Jesus. Jesus gives that power if a person is prepared well. Some of the churches have ministers and priests that have this authority and power, but many of them have fallen far short of the consciousness of one who mediates God for people. A priest is a mediator between God and human beings. Priests that are trained have been empowered to unite you with God if you work with them confidently and humbly. They have the rights given to them to bring you the body and blood of Jesus. They can heal your illnesses, awaken you from your spiritual sleep, and bring you into the illumination, the light of Christ. They can guide you into union with God and establish you powerfully on the spiritual path as disciples of the Masters Jesus and Mary. They have given their lives to God. They have been transformed and changed in the process of their training and spiritual work. They have let the teachers love them and heal them of all the myriad of problems that beset human beings before they return home to God.

Only a transformed priest is conscious enough to perform the sacrament of communion. They have been given the power of the word in being able to change the bread and wine into the body and blood of Jesus Christ. The word they have been given allows them to speak in God's place in all the areas that pertain to coming home to God. In our order, deacons can baptize and perform a modified form of the communion, called missionary communion. They ask Jesus to change the bread and wine into his body and blood, whereas the priest has the power to change it through the authority given to them directly. Deacons are part of the ministry and may at some point enter into training for the priesthood, so they work under the authority of the teachers and priests of this order.

People have such little faith that they cannot imagine or believe that the transmutation of bread and wine into Jesus' body and blood is possible. They feel it is commemorative and merely a form of remembering what Jesus did. They don't believe it can actually and realistically be done by speaking it so. At our Centers of Light, people can receive blessings that prove to them the power of the word. When you receive a blessing from one of our priests, you will feel something, and may go through big changes. Often, so much power and love move inside a person that afterwards they are completely different. Sometimes people will even look physically different following a blessing and will know something really, actually happened to them. Because the reality of a blessing is so real, with the spirit moving in a blessing to change feelings and conditions is so powerful, it is not hard to believe that the word of a priest can also change bread and wine into the flesh and blood of Jesus.

Please examine now whether you feel God is real. Ask yourself if you think Jesus or Mary is real. If you need to know for sure, why don't you ask them to come to you and make their presence felt to you in a way that will be unmistakable and undeniable. Be courageous and ask them to do this for you so that you will know for sure. There are forces in the mind of the world that will gobble up your beautiful, powerful, loving experiences and destroy them in a few hours unless you are very vigilant and possessive of them. You need to hold them sacred or they will fade under the influence of so much doubt, fear and scoffing minds in the world. The world mind does not want Jesus and Mary to be real because if they are real, then the world will be shown up as severely disobedient and out of balance. If you have ever tried telling your friends or relatives about a spiritual experience you have had, you probably found them getting frightened as if something was wrong with you. The more you tell them and the more real it gets for you, the more frightened they become. It is difficult to reconcile because they claim great support and love for you, but they apparently have not had such experiences and have no idea where to place them in their minds since they have not had them themselves. So they fear them because they are unknown to them.

What Jesus said comes to mind:

> This is the condemnation, that people loved darkness rather than light, because their deeds were evil. They do not come to the light. They hate the light. But now they have no excuse for their darkness, because light

has come into the world (John 3:19).

Jesus was saddened because he could have healed anything they were experiencing and he offered everything to anyone regardless of how bad their condition was. He had power over all illnesses, whether of soul, mind or body and he demonstrated thousands of healings to those who had just a small bit of faith in him and in the possibility.

Through daily communion, you can start the process of healing in your heart and soul. You can begin to come into union with God on a daily basis and slowly and certainly you will find the problems you once struggled with are no longer present in your consciousness. Your life will be changed in hundreds of ways that you cannot imagine now. This is happening for our students, and because of their experience, most of them would not think of missing a communion or miss praying to God each day. Communion involves getting down on your knees before God and allowing yourself to become completely empty of any concepts about who you are or how good you are. You let everything go and you open in humility to God to fill you and heal you and make you like God.

This is an experiential path, where inner work is our responsibility. Inner work means going within to find who you are. You go within to let go of the outer identifications so that you can start a conscious relationship to God at the center of your being. God is waiting for you. Do you want to know God? Do you want God to love you? Then go within and empty yourself of trying to show God how smart you are. Stop trying to show God how pretty you are, how strong you are and all the other ego things you are likely to think about. God knows you better than that and God recognizes only those things in you that are like God. The rest of the stuff, God ignores and wants you to let those things go.

"Now that you have seen, do you understand what the Eucharist is? It is my Heart that I distribute to you. I could not make you a greater or more loving gift.

If, when you received Communion, you were able to see Me, who give you my Heart, wouldn't you be moved? But faith should be very strong and charity very strong in order for you to see this. This mental vision should not constitute an exceptional gift by Me. It should constitute the rule, the sweet rule. And it would be the rule if you were really my disciples.

Then you would see me and hear me saying the words of consecration over the Bread and the Wine, breaking and distributing the Bread, offering it to you with my very own Hands. My priest would disappear, because I would superimpose Myself upon them to say to you, 'Here is the Body of the Lord Jesus Christ, my Body, which is to preserve you for eternal life.' And in the light of love you would see that I offer you my very Heart, the super perfect part of my most perfect Body, the part from which Charity itself flows forth.

I have done this out of love for you: I have given Myself. And I have done this for you today: I have lifted the veil of the Mystery and brought you to know how I come to you, how I give myself to you, what I give you that is mine, even if you are unable to see and understand" (*The Notebooks, 1943*, p. 99).

Chapter Eighteen

In the Silence

There is a lot of noise in peoples' heads, thoughts going miles per hour through the brain, filling up the head. I sometimes think people would be lonely if there was nothing going on up there, if there was no stream of thoughts running by, if it was quiet and still. We have been taught from childhood to think thoughts, and to gain honor, praise and acclaim for how we put those thoughts together and how our intellect works. In our educational process a high price is placed on thinking and getting the right answer. This does not amount to a hill of beans in comparison to a relationship with God. In fact, you have to quiet down a great deal just to get to the place where you can be still enough to feel God inside you. You might be fascinated to know that our students are getting real answers from God. When you ask a question and listen, you get an answer. That is true because God is talking to people all the time. The trouble comes when two or three people are talking at the same time. You can't hear any of the parties because of the overload. You hear nothing. That is what is happening with all the noise in the world. There are the sounds of birds, car horns, electricity and generators, the hum of heaters and air conditioners, the streetlights and wind. Then we hear the crashing sound of breathing, blood being pumped and nerve cells firing in the body. If you ever have listened inside, with a stethoscope, you can hear the gurgling of the intestines, the sloshing of the blood back and forth out of the heart, all the pumps and synapsing of chemicals and proteins moving around. It is very loud in there. You have to still all of this in order to hear the voice of God, to hear the presence of the stillness.

You are a created being. You did not create yourself. An intelligent and loving being fashioned and put you together. If you do not know that yet, you are in for quite a surprise. Somebody cared enough about you to make you an organized, orderly functioning being. The way God put you together works, and it is pretty amazing that your body works and lasts for ninety years. Cars do not last that long. Human beings have not been able to do that. With our vast intelligence, we cannot make things last very long before they break. There is something at the core of your being that is God. You are a cell in the mind of God, with the full capacity and perfection of God. The direction within is also the direction up in vibration. Within is up. Higher in vibration is within you. You have to quiet the outer noise and distractions, if you want to find your core, the essence of your own being, the soul and God Self. All the wise ones have spent time in meditation and silence trying to get to that connection within. They call it the still small voice, and the soundless sound. It's the kind of sound that when you hear it you know instantly what it is saying and what it means. You did not create it or put it there. The answer popped up into your mind. People have described it in different ways; you just intuitively perceive it right away, in its simple form. This is the divine being that you are. It has nothing to do with the human mind, emotions or body.

What happens here on this planet is you have to squeeze yourself down to such a small hunk of flesh that it is like being in a prison. It is like being in hell. Hell is really a misconception. It is an experience where you misperceive reality and you exist in a false reality. It is commonly accepted as a place where human beings feel limited and separate from God. They choose to be disconnected. Even after you die, you go to a place of disconnection confined by your misconception until you change that concept. It is not a place so much as an experience.

We go into the inner silence to commune with the divine being that made us. Actually we go into the inner silence to be loved. The first thing you see is light, and the next thing you feel is love as you move close to it. Your hell, your misconception of life, will prevent you from love. Social life demands love from other people, from the outside world. You rarely ever look inside yourself for love. This is why we call this the inner path. It is path, not a destination. It's not a place you arrive at, it's a process you go through to become closer to God. Jesus said, "Know you not that you are Gods?" and "The dominion of God is within you." This is the truth that all teachers teach. It is totally literal that God is inside and that the dominion of God is within. All mystics go within and silence their thinking when they meditate. They stop scratching, still their body, and forget the consciousness of the body for a few minutes. They go into the place where they are communicating with God and God talks to them. They see God. Risking an unpopular opinion, I have to say that the Buddhists don't go far enough. They only go into a kind of a peaceful state but almost never get deep enough to find God inside. God is inside all human beings, regardless of tradition or races. Most people are not looking for or thinking of God. Most people don't even like the idea of God because they have a parent problem, projecting the wrath and punishments they received from caregivers unto God and assuming God will act that way towards them. They don't know anything about God. It is all concepts in their head. What I know about God is that God is love, and there is no condemnation. God is joy and bliss. God completely sees and knows you and is vastly superior in intelligence than any created being. God is higher than you could ever imagine, as well as more real, more loving and deeper. That is what you find when you go into the inner silence.

Here is the problem with meditation: if you don't know yourself very well, the first thing you see when you go into meditation is all your darkness. All of a sudden, your thoughts turn wild and you cannot keep them quiet. You are distracted, itchy, and you cannot keep still. Your mind is racing fast as you flit from idea to idea. When you get still and forget about your body, the first things that come up in your mind are all your darkness and negative feelings. All the history of negative feelings and criticisms that others put on you is all stuck in there. These are bad feelings that others spoke to you. People are cowards; they resist facing their own negative feelings and thoughts and stop meditating. They are scared off and will not be able to heal.

When you first begin to meditate, it is like when you latch onto a relationship, and try to get someone to love you. The first thing that happens is that all the unresolved stuff from your childhood comes up. You act that out on the unlucky person. It happens so quickly that you are not aware that it is happening. As soon as someone wants to get close, they have this job to heal you from the past. That is the same thing that happens in meditation. All the fears and wounds rise up in your consciousness as you try to get closer to God.

At this stage, God is still a speculation. You might feel God, but you cannot see God. You are not in direct relationship with God yet. You are only surmising and anticipating a relationship. You cannot trust it yet and are only hopeful that God is real. You still have a lot of work to do. As Bob Dylan wrote, "You're going to have to trust somebody. You're going to have trust in the devil or trust in the Lord, but you're going to have trust someone." You have to go through the process, the journey to find God. It is a risk. Change causes suffering and purification if you are going to be transformed. It is a bold thing to say, "I know God and I can take you there." That is pretty weird. It is also unpopular. We are either crazy or we really do have this goldmine of love we want to introduce you to. I am practical and not about to do anything that does not work. It is very simple. It worked for me and it worked for a group of other people, so what I tell you will work for you. If you have more faith, you might just do what I say because I say it. That is what is so exciting about having a spiritual community, because may other people are having these experiences. You can talk to them about it. I am lazy about doing things that don't work. I do not want to waste any time. I will tell you the most direct route rather than have you spin your wheels going around and around the mountain pretending to be on the spiritual path. Most of the paths just trudge around the mountain taking forever. Many teachers talk about a path but do not know how to take you there. We know how.

At first you have to silence the mind of the world and the minds of the people around you. You have to silence and re-

nounce it. Later you will have to renounce your own thinking. If you look at your thinking right now, it is wild. You
think random things every few seconds. This undermines
your progress. Every negative thought, every insecure or
doubtful feeling is a worried mind. Each inconsiderate snap-
ping or porcupine poking of another person because you are
feeling bad stops your growth. When you sit on the bench
and assess the traffic, thinking about how far you have come
and how far you have to go, warming the bench with your
gluttonous thoughts, you are not moving. You have to move
on down the road instead of having a shifting butt meditation. If you are not moving, then nothing is happening. You
are dreaming of action and not acting; dreaming of progress and not progressing. Time marches on, so if you are sit-
ting on the bench of life, you are going backwards. This is
why Jesus said "You cannot serve two masters." You cannot serve the world mind and God at the same time. They
are totally opposed to each other. They do not operate in
the same space or in the same energy. One goes backwards
into stuckness and concrete mind, and the other moves into
light, spirit and love. One takes love and courage, while the
other is doubt and fear.

You have probably had the experience of picking up a random lustful thought passing through your mind, a thought
you usually do not have in your head. You picked that up
from someone around you who thought that. Ask yourself,

"Do I normally have a thought like this?" If you don't usually have this thought, then there is a demon suggesting that thought or someone nearby is thinking it. People even say, "I don't know what came over me." We have the language for it. "I was completely beside myself." Ask yourself, "Is this a thought I usually think?" If it is, then it is coming from inside you. But if it is not from you, say to Jesus, "Take this thing away. It is garbage; I do not want it; I reject it; I do not accept it." You could also send it back to the one who sent it out.

You should pray for protection while you work so you do not pick up people's negative stuff. It can slip in within seconds, so you have to be fairly conscious of yourself to know the influences you are hanging around with all the time. You could find yourself in a mood in the afternoon, and you don't know when it happened. You have to track it back to when it started. Was I in a mood at break time? Before lunch? Okay, what happened around that time? When did the mood start, and who was involved? You need to quicken the time when you find out what the problem was so that you catch it before it infests you and takes over with its toxic vibration. You have to catch things faster than that.

You will be wise if you go into meditation with some protection from God, so you do not scare yourself half to death. If you have never looked at your life to examine it, you are going to see a bunch of garbage in there. The wounds of the past, the hurts and sadness that you never looked at will be the first things that come up for review. If you are slippery, you might blame them on everyone outside you. But if you are wise, you will see that these are inside you and have contaminated you. You can review who influenced you, maybe parents, and then clean it up and fix it. If it's contaminated, then it's contaminated. If it's negative and it feels bad, then you should not want it. You need to understand it, but you need to get it out of there. It needs to be healed.

You need a guide up the mountain of attainment. Otherwise you will meander or go down instead of up. You need someone who says, "Oh no, no, no, don't sit on that rock." You might be tired, but the teacher will say, "You are just about to overcome something right now, so do not sit down." You need someone who can tell you, "Yes, that is an alluring path, but don't take that one, because you are going to wind up in a heap of trouble." Even if you take the most difficult way, it might be out of pride. The teacher will warn you, "Do not take that most difficult road or you will get too discouraged. You are the kind of person that needs quick successes as your temperament is too weak at present to take the hard way."

If you receive guidance in meditation and you are not sure it is real, check it out with your priest or teacher. You can be easily tricked or deluded by putting the message in there yourself. It takes a great deal of practice to become proficient at getting guidance. Our students test their guidance with a priest or teacher, so there is a check and balance system in place. You can get in the way by wanting too little, and you can get in the way by wanting too much. Your mind is tricky and might lobby for an answer that supports your desire. This is called being biased. You might be resisting a "no" and lobbying for a "yes." You learn to get yourself out of the way by training yourself to be willing to go either way with complete surrender and enthusiasm. You tell yourself that you will do whatever God tells you to do. You could say to your spiritual teachers, "I am going to place my decision in your hands and do what you tell me." Since a real teacher knows what you should do, it will save you a great deal of heartache and pain. When you are praying for guidance, you should ask God to really get through to you so you really hear it. You need to be out of the way to avoid biasing the answer. Most of you are not spiritually developed enough to be able to get clear guidance, because you have so many concepts. You have some work to do to get to the place where you have no fear, no anger, and are willing to be led by God without putting your own 16 cents in there. That should be humbling.

As a created being, you have some portion of God's intelligence; you could have as much as God gives you if you were out of the way. Jesus said, "I and my Father-Mother are one." You could have that, too, but you would have to have given up your life. Jesus said, "Not my will but yours be done." It can happen if it is not about you anymore. If you are courageous and willing to express God's energy, God's love, then you would have given up doing your own thing. Fear, worry, anger, pride and insecurity are blocks to God's expression. There is a whole process involved, which is why you need a teacher. The teacher asks, "What is your attitude today?" You might answer, "Well, I feel better than other people." The teacher responds, "Oh. Do you need me to get the nose pulley installed for you? A pulley is fastened to the ceiling and the other end strapped to your nose. That is what it looks like when you think that way."

When you think you should be exempt from hard things and what others are required to go through on the spiritual path, when you're exempt from the disciplines that are necessary to go deeper in God because you are smarter, more capable and more spiritual, then you may be in danger of striving for gifts and graces that you do not deserve. Those are the nose pulley gifts. Every sin has an odor. Insecurity has its odor, doubt has its odor, worry has an odor, anger has an odor, fear has an odor and pride has a big odor. Anybody good at sniffing things out can smell them. Two parts per million. People who are murderers have covered over the God within them so much that their conscience is almost dead. They are acting out their hell and completely out of touch with the feeling of right and wrong. They have no pangs of conscience if they hurt somebody, and there's no feeling of remorse for any time they disrespect another person. We would say that they are like a sarcophagus buried under many feet of earth. They're dense and cut off from themselves so much that they can't feel the divine spark at all. If you felt a vestige of God's presence inside, you would have a little love for people and some concern about whether you were being mean or not. You would feel it. It would hurt you if you acted that way. Some people are so angry that their crimes are in proportion to the abuse they receive in childhood. The more beaten up, hurt, abused and neglected in childhood, the more violent the crime later on. That is how Hitler was formed. Hitler had a dad who beat him every day when he came home, and a mom who was too helpless and weak to stand up for him or to say anything about it. At 13, Hitler stopped showing any more tears to his father, but buried the rage inside, repressing it. Later when he heard that his father had a grandfather who was Jewish, all of the anger was unleashed against the Jews because of that abuse. If you want to create a Hitler, beat the hell out of a kid and don't protect him, and don't have anybody around that cares about him, and you'll turn a person into somebody like that. That is how it works.

Many people have been mistreated or neglected and so have a great deal of healing work to do in order to get back to being with God. You cannot heal if you are distancing yourself from the way God made you, because of the hurts you had from the parents. In our spiritual school, the first thing we notice people doing on the way to healing is to project all their parent stuff onto God and the priests. That is the reason we do the psychological work. We've seen it over and over again. We deal with this directly, and we won't side-step it. There have been no spiritual schools or orders on the planet that have ever done this except us. We are doing it and not avoiding it. Some resist doing this work, but many want to do it. The ones who do the work are in another world compared to all other spiritual workers. They are healed inside and integrated. They are not running away to the spiritual life to get away from pain. You have to go through the healing of all that pain to get to the spiritual life. In other churches, a person can get ordained without any personal healing work and then possibly act out their wound on their victims. That is what happens if those problems are not healed. You have to leaven the whole lump.

Psychotherapy can help, but most therapists have no spiritual sight and many do not believe in God. They help with communication skills and behavior change and do some minor healing of wounds. They are not able to do the deep work that getting close to God can do. Our newer students have to clean out the garbage and personal problems first. You cannot hope to receive the deeper teachings until there is a place cleared out to receive and hold those. You have to pay the price for that. The price to pay is a clean mind locking in to God, and then you will get the deeper teachings. That is how it works. We are not playing around with these things. Many teachings were given to the Apostles that were never written down and were never given to the rest of the people. Why? Because they could not handle it. If may sound unfair to you, but there were twelve apostles. One was a liar and a murderer and only three were permitted to go with Jesus up to Mount Tabor to witness his illumination. The same three were allowed to be there with Jesus when he was suffering and taking on everyone's sins at Gethsemane. Peter, James and John were the only ones spiritually evolved enough to be close to Jesus when he was doing something so powerfully spiritual. They were the only ones who could understand it. The other apostles would never have thought this unfair and would not have questioned it. They knew Jesus, knew that everything he did was perfect and they had implicit faith in him.

Most of you are not even close to that level of intimacy with Jesus and Mary. This might sting your pride. Your pride keeps you out of relationship with God. Whatever you think you know is going to be a detriment to you somewhere along the path. Students are led into a place of unknowing and taken through an experience they can't preview. Why? Because their mind would mess with it and actually block the experience. On this path, you are taken to a place you have not experienced yet. In a lateral move you could see across, but you can't see above or ahead. If you think you can, it is just pride, flatulence of the brain. You have to be willing to be led into an experience you do not know yet. That is in the silence and in meditation where Jesus will drag you through to an experience. You are led around in the dark, your own darkness. I sometimes pull you through an experience not mentioning anything about the steps, because it is not your business. One of my teachers said, "Understanding is the booby prize." Understanding is what you get AFTER you go through something. Then you are a divine being and can express your divinity as an immortal soul. But most of you are acting like a frog with warts. You have fallen from grace. It is hard to be a disciple. The freedom you gain from following God, the world has no idea about.

Intuition comes out of the blue. You cannot call it forth to inspire you. You have to wait for it. When your mind is disciplined, you can ask for help directly and get it through guidance. That is different. You have to be able to connect and get out of the way and listen. Then you have to be willing to do what the guidance says. Intuition is random and primitive by comparison. When people ask me questions, I don't just randomly come up with ideas. I am not able to function like that. I have to know what God says on any given matter. I need to know for sure. You will not be clear if you are constricted and afraid. If you have a concept of how things are supposed to go, you have pride all over it trying to figure it out or trying to get it right. Relax and get simple. You need to approach the crowd like Jesus did: "Here I am, without one plea, I can of my own self do nothing." That establishes your baseline with God and with Jesus. I of my own self can do nothing. It means whatever gets done through me is God doing it. That is the adventure of the spiritual path. You do not always know what is going to happen, but it will be good. You cannot control it. All of you control freaks out there; nothing will happen if you try to control everything, because you are already managing a half a step ahead. God will not cooperate with you if you try to lead.

It is important that you figure out what you want, but make sure you leave how it happens to God. Don't mess with that part. That is not your business. You are creators and can create a good picture of what you want. It might be just a trial run. Do the best you can with it, give that to God and let God figure out how to get it to you. You might get a pleasant surprise of exactly what you want, or it might be better than that. As soon as you get what you asked for, you might say, "That was a great idea, but I do not want that." You learn, and now you can change and get what you do want. You are still a creator. There are other chances to learn what is important to you. Do it again and practice until you get it just right. You practice until you get closer and closer approximations to the desired goal. You change as you grow, and what you like today you probably will not like ten years from now. Occasionally God will not give you something because it is essentially bad for you. Stop being passive. You might feel drawn to something, so ask for it and take responsibility for it. As soon as you put a thought out, it goes into the mind of God and is going to come back to you. God wants you to make choices.

Chapter Nineteen

Do You Know Peace?

Do you know what peace is? Is peace an experience you have all the time? Once you experience it, does it stay? If you are experiencing peace, you would not want anything. You would already have it. You would not need someone else to take care of things for you because you would take care of those things yourself without any anxiety. If peace was in your blood, it would be in your cells. Peace flowing through you would go everywhere, even in your heart, your thoughts. Do you worry? That is not peace. Do you get angry? That is not peace. Do you fear things will go wrong? That is not peace. Do you want what others have? That is not peace. Do you hope that God will strike the ones who do wrong and recompense those that make trouble for other people on this planet? That is not peace.

There is no peace in retaliation or paying people back for wrongs committed. There is no peace if your heart wants others to pay. There is no peace if you want God to strike down your enemies or wake people up in a harsh manner.

There is no peace in anger and retaliation. "Vengeance is mine, says the Lord." God is the one who will judge the living and the dead.

Nervousness and anxiety have no peace. It is worrying about the future. If your mind is out in the future, you are picturing events that haven't occurred and your heart is out there. You are fantasizing about what might happen or scaring yourself about some disaster you are creating in your head. This fearful practice takes you away from peace and from your trust in God. Is God real? Is God watching over you or not? Can you rely on it or must you constantly oversee how God is doing at keeping you safe? You can hear people say, "What I would not do to get a moments peace." Or "What do I have to do to get some peace?" "I just need a little peace and quiet." You can create agitation or you can create peace. But as soon as you look outside and watch what other people do and fail to do, you lose your peace. If the outer world must conform to your desires in order for you to have peace, then you will never have peace. When you no longer look to see how people are doing or how the world is accommodating you, then you are on the way to finding peace. Even so, if no one bothers you and the world is fine, you still might have a battle of worry and anger and fear going on inside you that prevents you from being at peace.

Recall to your mind's eye a time when you were so still and

so empty of any ambition or striving that time stood still for a few moments. There was nothing to worry about and nowhere to go. You were free from plans and memories, just completely absorbed in the present moment. Time stood still because time ceased to exist. Every moment was filled with life and there was nothing else but that one moment. In that moment, you were in bliss and there was peace. Peace is the space between there and then. You should visit there more often. You should hang out in that space so that it grows inside you and becomes full. That space between there and then is the moment when grace and blessings can flow from the Infinite into the finite. The human being opens and God fills you completely. In the Order of Christ Sophia, we meditate to lose our consciousness of the body while focusing on the soul and the light. We relax all outer awareness and still our thinking mind to focus only on our subject. Many times we focus on light or God or Jesus and Mary. This focus takes us off ourselves and our little world of concerns and puts our consciousness on something much vaster and fuller. God becomes our focus and peace flows through in waves of richness.

Peace is the blessing Jesus gave whenever he entered any place or space. He would say, "Peace be with you." Obviously, Jesus thought this was very important. Peace is the prerequisite for God to be able to act. If you are stressed out, God cannot act. If you are anxious and pushing for a result, God cannot act because you show by your thoughts and actions that you do not have faith in what God will bring or in what you have asked. You have to relax if you want to have the blessings of God. If you think you have to do everything by yourself and with your own personal intelligence and capabilities, then you have a misconception about God. You still think God is out there someplace. God is inside you. God is the only life that can act through you. You are nothing without God. Only in this peace could Jesus perform a healing or teach a lesson. Even if the people were agitated, it was within Jesus' peace that these things were done. Jesus was simply confident in God acting and moving through him and that is how all the healings were accomplished. Jesus said what he wanted and it happened. You can also come to the place where you will be able to say what you want and it will be done.

You must be at peace if you can ever hope to know God. The world is not at peace, if you haven't noticed. There are over 25 wars going on at any one time on the earth. People are killing each other left and right. There have been American troops in Germany since WWII and in Korea and Vietnam since those wars supposedly ended. War energy does not stop on this planet. The U.S. is responsible for many of the wars under the rationale that we are peace-keeping forces. We have almost never been a proponent of peace and have actually interfered in the governments of hundreds of countries in the name of democracy. In this country, during the years 2005 through 2011, there were over 16,500 murders each year. Most of these homicides were between people that knew each other personally. We are not a peaceful people. We are angry, aggressive and mean. We justify our violence with self-righteousness and pride, willfully disregarding the rights of others to hold differing opinions and religious ideas. This is not peace. If the U.S. is not actively in war like we are now, we are always paranoid that someone is creating weapons that will be more powerful than ours and we are constantly inventing more and more destructive weapons to annihilate enemies. This is completely against the Ten Commandments. The 5th commandment is "You shall not kill." Murder, even in war, is killing, so it is not Christian and not of God. There is no rationale that can justify it and no amount of selling the people on the dangers of the enemy that can justify our aggressive actions.

> Jesus says: "Whoever kills love kills peace. The more alive love is, the more alive peace is. Do you want the measure of how a being loves? Observe whether or not he has peace with himself. Whoever loves acts rightly. In acting rightly he experiences no disturbance. This is valid for all forms of love" (*The Notebooks 1943*, p. 160)

You need to know that peace is the opposite of building weapons and perfecting the technology of war. Peace is mercy and love. Peace is consideration for other people and accepting people with their warts and their differences. Peace is not angry and does not react out of emotions. Peace is a way of life that has to be practiced in order for a person to become a master of peace. Jesus Christ was a master of peace. He said something that few people comprehend.

> "Do not think that I have come to bring peace on the earth; I have not come to bring peace, but a sword. For I have come to set a man against his father, and a daughter against her mother, and a daughter-in-law against her mother-in-law; and one's foes will be the members of one's own household. Whoever loves father or mother more than me is not worthy of me; and whoever loves son or daughter more than me is not worthy of me; and whoever who does not take the cross and follow me is not worthy of me." (Matthew 10: 34).

The division between those who follow a spiritual path and those who do not is becoming more obvious. You cannot bargain with righteousness and obedience to God. There are no half-way measures. It is a hard road to travel to be in peace and to love God above all other loves. In this world, family is a god that is worshipped by billions. They have no higher god than family. And yet Jesus is extremely clear. Do you think you can really be a Christian if you pick and choose which of Jesus' teachings you like and which you don't? The sad fact is that the majority of people have never read Jesus' teachings, or worse, the ministers don't teach what Jesus taught. God is first and following Jesus is the way to put God first. Worshipping the family is ridiculous and has no part in the way of Christ. You have to honor your parents and respect them for the love they gave in having you and raising you, but you do not override common sense if they were mean or abusive or neglecting. If you follow the way of Christ, you will have to let go many of the traditions and practices of family since they are not of God. Following Jesus and Mary places you at odds with established customs and family patterns since you will have one love that is higher than your DNA contributors. In fact, the main persecutors of the real followers of Jesus will be their families because they do not want you to be further along spiritually than they are, and they definitely don't want you out of the family control of what is expected of you. You have to be at peace even if the people around you are not at peace.

Jesus also said, "But I say unto you, love your enemies, and pray for those who persecute you." There is nothing in here about praying for their demise or retaliating with aggression or violence. There is love and praying only, no matter what is done to you. Jesus goes on to teach: "You have heard that the ancients were told, 'You shall not commit murder.' But I say to you that everyone who is angry with his brother shall be guilty before the court." Even anger is not permissible if you are following Jesus. Anger leads to violence because it gives vent to your pride and stimulates your fear.

You have to strive to the place where you entrust your life and your future into the hands of God. God will take care of you whether you have a body or not, whether you live or die, whether your body is violently abused and killed or whether it is preserved for a ripe old age. The timing of your life is in God's hands and the sooner you accept that, the better for this world. Do no harm and do no violence to anyone. Do not react if violence is done to you. Forgive and pray for the wayward, ignorant person who was rageful or inconsiderate. They are spiritually uneducated and need your prayers and your good example. There is nothing on this earth that is worth very much, even your precious flesh body. God will provide you with another one if the one you have is damaged. But I want to caution you not to disregard or mistreat your body, as it is the vessel God gave you in order to shine the Light and be an example of God here.

Jesus says:

"What peace?.... I said that to obtain true peace, and not a pause in the war, it was necessary to remove from your midst what was fornication with Satan. I have said so through the mouths of my saints, and I have had my Mother say so. For decades I have been repeating this, and for decades you have been insisting on that. I have told you so with urgent words in these recent times. But you have not changed. Rather, you have increasingly made fornication with Satan your way of life.

You have preferred everything else to God. And this God whom you invoke in the hour of fear is such a distant, unknown Being for you that if you were consistent, you should not even invoke or blaspheme any longer, for you have drifted so far away from Him. Indeed, even your invocations are blasphemy, for you call Him with lips sullied with filth, for you invoke Him while you are still one with Satan, for you dare to mix his Holy Name with your plans for crime.

Peace has been promised to men of good will. Christ came to bring Peace. But if you send Christ away and your will is not good, how can you have peace? You have pauses. But they are nothing but intervals between one slaughter and another, to give time for your spirits, sold to Satan, to learn new doctrines of death from him and new instruments of destruction.
Death to souls and death to the flesh. Destruction of spirits and destruction of things. Your growth in Satan is impressive. In a short while, you will have reached the mature age in which he will no longer have any-

thing to teach you, and then Hell will be able to give birth to its son – the Antichrist – for the times will be ripe and men will have deserved to know the horror preceding the end'" (*The Notebooks 1943,* p. 464).

When you taste of peace, you will know from experience how to be in life. Peace will become your calling card because peace will flow through you in your words and your breath. Your presence will bring peace into any room you enter and people will know that the presence of God is there with you. Peace in your heart is the only guarantee that you will be helping God, Jesus and Mary with their mission on this planet. Peace is the discipline of not being where you are not, not being ahead of yourself or kicking yourself for past mistakes. Peace is the eternal existence between there and then.

Chapter Twenty

Divine Feminine: Following Your Intuition

I
t is probably a bit strange for a human being in a male
body to be speaking about the divine feminine. In fact,
it may be such a difficult topic that language barely de-
scribes the reality of what we are talking about. If it is divine,
then it is of God. Since it is the feminine aspect of God, then
it holds a receptive place, a still quality that is strong and full.
But what is this divine feminine really?

It is describable in images and metaphors like a fluid substance, moist and wet, but teeming with life. In this watery
substance new life begins nourished by its own nature, fed
by its own vital essence. We began in the water of the am-
niotic fluid. We breathed this fluid in and out of our lungs.
This water is the basis of our life force moving in and out of
us, enclosing us and permeating each cell. The divine feminine has the quality of holding us in its embrace, sustaining
us and providing our every need. It gives us its complete attention and provides us with everything necessary to support
our life development.

Infinite containment is the attribute of the divine feminine. Held in the arms of the great one, we are sustained with all the energy, power and force we may ever need. Our every wish and desire is answered affirmatively. The divine being responds by giving us everything we need, completely supporting the life within us in our striving to fulfill and find ourselves. Each thought of ours is known and sensed by the divine feminine. The nature of this receptive field of being is to take care of each need, causing an influx of substance, grace, life and love to flow to the human beings, who are gods in embryo. We are sustained in infinite love, held within the ever widening view of this great being whose attention keeps us alive. If the divine feminine ceased to hold us in this perpetual embrace, we would fly out of existence, cut off from that connection. We are contained within the consciousness of this intelligence, this divine presence.

For males, the divine feminine is at once very attractive and appealing, yet at the same time awesome and overwhelming. It is that embrace that may suffocate your freedom. It may strip you of the misconception that you control anything, or that you can accomplish anything of yourself. If you are contained and encompassed on every side, from all directions at once, where are you able to stand and what exactly can you take credit for? This aspect of the divinity is the power of stillness magnified to many times more uncomfortable than you are used to. This stillness and receptivity causes you to take full responsibility for whatever you create, while giving you no way to understand how much love it takes for this great presence to allow you to have anything and everything you want.

In the view of the world and the unenlightened, you want things to be easy, so you can take them by force and take credit for getting them once received. From the perspective of the divine feminine, you are given everything you need, but you cannot control it and you did not create it. You are only responsible for the making of the request. From a materialistic point of view, if you desire to take credit for everything that happens, you will ultimately have to cut off the divine presence in order to remove any competition in your field of action. You might mistakenly imagine that all of the things that you accomplish and create are from your own finite fountain of energy, and that your creativity originates in your thinking. You are in danger of fencing yourself off from the divine, and imagining that you are the ruler of all that you see and know.

If, on the other hand, you allow and accept the divine feminine to hold you, support you and fill you with good things, then you grow in leaps and bounds. The grace that attends your life carries a presence of hope and joy that sustains you. This energy emanates from you and causes others to want to be near you, to enjoy being with you because you are connected to something deeper, wider and more powerful than you could generate within your own confinement, with just yourself alone. For females, there is an easy association and identification with the divine feminine, because the body nature of women is much like the divine feminine. There is a tendency for women to live in the body, complacent in the here and now, which makes the divine presence more of a physical experience. You might settle for this bodily sensation of the divine feminine – devotional in its nature and posing as worship of God – as enough of a connection. But experience of the divine feminine for women must go much deeper to the place where outer conclusions, dogmatic assertions and opinionated reveries are rejected and released. The inner wisdom pulls you inside to a much deeper place than the naturally beautiful, peaceful but complacent nature of the resting physical energy. Inside in the stillness, you will find no identification with the body even though your body will grow stronger and more alive. Your approach to the divine feminine floods you with true feeling, true awareness and real understanding. You are not alone and when you begin to know that, you begin to say things with real authority, real knowing and real power. Your word begins to have strength and begins to move things in the material world, not with ego, but with profound love.

It takes a bit of work, study and concentration to come into union with the divine feminine. The concentration is important because we have to center our focus and attention to the point where we can pass through the gate of this experience. The intensity of our longing for the experience must be strong enough to connect to that which we desire. This is the only holy desire: union with God. We cannot expect to just sit in a relaxed state and hope to meet the divine feminine. We must boldly move towards it, expecting to meet it and be known by it.

The divine feminine is the holy place where the realness of your true nature is completely accepted. You are embraced at the most basic and true level. You are accepted for the true nature you have inside, in the soul and Self. True acceptance is what the divine feminine has for everyone. No conditions, no qualifications. The divine feminine is the place where heart meets heart. It is the energy that allows the true nature of one to interact and connect with the true nature of another. There are no considerations that would make possible a separation, no excuses that would prevent us from entering into that holy respect and honoring of another. Our hearts would burn inside us with the acknowledgment that at the level of God being, WE ARE ONE.

It seems necessary to say a few things about the divine masculine in order to not be one-sided. Understand that the divine masculine and the divine feminine are blended and complementary within the great being of God. No part of God is in conflict with any other part of God. These energies move like day follows night and activity follows rest. In The Book of Changes, the I CHING, the masculine nature of God is depicted creative, energizing, ascending and of the heavens, while the feminine nature of God is depicted as receptive, descending and of the earth. One is the active, generating phase and the other is the quiet, healing phase of God's being. One is not possible without the other. The divine masculine is the intensity of the great one wanting something to take place. In the Gospel of John, it is "In the beginning was the Word." The great being spoke the word that contained all possibilities and that energy penetrated the emptiness and started creation. The decision was held in love and honor by the divine feminine, contained in a holy presence and supported by a complete acceptance.

The divine masculine is the part of God that initiates something new and unexpected into being. It changes things, it starts things into action, it stops things and lifts conditions by knowing what it wants. The divine masculine is able to say "no" to conditions and completely change things in accord with the new energy of the times. The divine masculine protects us when we get too far afield, too lost in our confusion, too ignorant of the source. Out of compassion and love, the divine masculine will intervene in the affairs of creation to bring back the cosmic pattern and renew the lost ones. This is the part of us that will protect us if we seek it out and want the help.

Chapter Twenty One

Men and Women, Sex and Honesty

We are born into flesh bodies that express a masculine or feminine gender. The flesh body of the male has a female spiritual body, and the flesh body of the female has a masculine spiritual body. The spiritual body is opposite the polarity of the flesh body because it is necessary in order to manifest on the material plane. This opposite polarity holds the physical and spiritual bodies together for their short duration here on earth. The spiritual body is the means through which the soul/Self can function in a physical body and vitalize it. When we get to earth, we have to learn to operate the physical vehicle we are living inside of and master its essential functions of thinking, feeling, talking, eating, digesting and learning. The electrical charge of the male body is positive and the electrical charge of the female body is negative.

In each person there is both male and female. In males, the feminine aspect is usually quieter and less expressed, and in females the masculine aspect is quieter and less expressed. We have access to the quieter part, but our bodies show the predominance of the gender we are born with. Do not make the mistake of thinking that because you are born into a particular gender that you have taken on that aspect and have already learned to master it. It may take some time and work to get to that level of mastery. If you think about it, you may have had a string of female lives and now are in a male body, so it will take some getting used to and adjusting to that expression. You came into the body you are in because of your soul's choice and for a particular reason. Do not fight it so much. You chose the gender because of experiences your soul needs and how you are supposed to do your mission on earth. Life can get very difficult if you get here and decide from your limited perspective that you are in the wrong body. From your soul's perspective, it is the perfect choice and the sooner you accept that, the sooner you will be able to make the most of your stay here in the physical world.

It is important to know that if you are female, you can call forth the dynamic, initiating, decisive and knowing side of your nature. If you are male, you need to be able to call on the sensitivity and gentleness of your nature. We have access to both qualities and both must be available in order to function perfectly. This will involve the uniting of the masculine and feminine energies within you, the blending of fire and water within oneself. Creation reveals the glory of God and the heavens declare God's handiwork. God contains both positive, masculine energies and receptive, feminine energies. God is neither male nor female, but both. Symbolically the sun and moon are said to copulate and come into union at the time of the full moon, where the sun gives the full light to the moon and the moon, in turn, reflects the fullness of the sun's light. This represents the conscious, active will of the sun and the subconscious, emotional response of the moon. The masculine energies within us think, and the feminine energies in us create from this energy. Masculine and feminine energies are a cosmic pattern.

The difficulty in identifying with the mass mind concept of masculine and feminine gender roles has made some people have trouble accepting their bodies. When that happens, there is usually an emotional or psychological reaction to one of the parents or some important person in life that makes you unable to identify with that person. Remember, God is not a fickle and mean parent figure. God is not trying to jerk us around by giving us a male or female body. Females do not have an advantage over the male because they are emotionally stronger. Males are not more favored by God because they have assumed control over females for most of history. Men and women are beginning to appreciate our essential equality and power.

Males and females function differently in terms of energy and creativity. They complement one another. The male polarity, wherever you find it, whether in males or females, is one of decision, action, initiation, protection and strength. The female polarity is receptivity, creativity, love, beauty, gentleness and relatedness. The male is the seed and the female is the creative, fertile field. The polarities balance and complement each other. The interior female or male which composes the spiritual body also balances and complements outer masculine and feminine energies. In every marriage, there are really three marriages, one between the physical bodies of the partners, another between the spiritual bodies of the partners, and the third between the masculine and feminine energies within each person. Two people become one flesh when matter and spirit come together in the love and commitment between a man and a woman.

Men have a lot of learning to do in relationship because they are not so sure they should have to talk about things very much. The stronger they feel in their world, the less they are inclined to share their feelings about themselves and things that are going on in their life. Our culture teaches boys that moms take care of everything and even interpret their body language for them before they learn how to communicate what is happening to them. An example: A little boy comes home from school and is whimpering and restraining some tears. Mom sees this and says, sympathetically, "What's wrong?" The boy says, "Nothing." She interprets this and over-helps as usual and says "Did that Johnny kid beat you up?" The boy whimpers, "Uh, huh." Mom gives him a hug and says lots of comforting words to him. What has the boy communicated really? Not very much. When the women around boys take care of the feeling side of things, is it any wonder that boys do not have the language or the need to communicate their feelings? When the boys grow up they will find a woman who will take care of things in the same way: they will want a woman who can read their feelings without a lot of excessive description and need for self-disclosure.

Men are looking for a woman who is a kind damsel, a maiden, innocent, pure, helpless and sensitive. In time, he can instruct her in the ways of the world, in how to take care of him, and he can tutor her into becoming the woman she has the potential to be, his ideal mother. In that way, he will finally be loved and he will help her put him in the place of God. As she learns under his guidance, he will reveal more of himself as he feels it is safe to show her who he is. In the meantime he is not very happy to have to feel deep emotions or feelings. He will make sure that she carries these feelings for him so he doesn't have to carry them or feel them so much. He is not sure what to do with them anyway. Feelings can be so uncomfortable and unmanageable. Feelings are not neat and ordered. They spread out all over the place, and you can't get anything done. The biggest fear he has is that he will have to reveal to her that he hasn't the slightest idea of what he is doing or where he is going. This vulnerability is the most uncomfortable thing for him to bear.

An example: A man comes home in a bad mood. She hears his mood in the way the car door slams. She can feel that things are not going well with him. He comes inside in a sour mood and begins to inflict it on her. She tries to be understanding and helpful. She uses her best method of empathy and understanding and he bats it away. He criticizes her and does not stop poking at her. There is nothing that she can do to help him at this point. He has gone down for the count. He is not sure why he feels bad and he has no idea when or how he began to feel this way. He just does, and he wants her to take this feeling over so he doesn't have to experience it any more. Remember, women are better at dealing with feelings and so she is an excellent recipient of what he can't understand anyway. He pokes at her meanly. She tries to love him and gradually she feels more and more attacked and hurt. If she cries or gets really angry, he stops completely. Then he feels perfectly fine. He then says that she should just get over it and states that he is done with it and has moved on, so why can't she? She is devastated and will take a few hours or even days to get her feathers all settled and feeling better.

The principle here is that he did not want those feelings, whatever they are. He wants her to carry them and deal with them for him. He waits to sting her with the poison of the mood and when she takes it on and gets angry or cries, he feels released of his mood and she carries it now. If a woman takes this kind of treatment, she is allowing him to keep from growing up. Women, don't do that for your man. Let him go through his own stuff and wait for him to get over it and communicate what was happening to him in a responsible way. He needs to deal with his own stuff and he needs to learn to talk about it responsibly without trying to get her to do all the emotional work.

For you men, take some time when you are in a bad mood and figure out when it started. It usually started several hurt feelings ago, maybe even five or six hits that you took. Then you felt that this last one put you over the top and you were really hurt. It just dawned on you. You were hurt the first four times and did not register it. You need to know how you feel that so that you are not blind-sided by situations. Then if you feel bad about something, you don't have to take it out on someone, like your wife or woman friend, you can speak about how you feel without inflicting your pain on someone else.

Undisciplined or irresponsible sexual behavior is a way for men to gain some release from their misconception that semen must be discharged to reduce the pressure. No one to date has ever died of lack of orgasm. I have interviewed a few emergency room physicians and they cannot attest to anyone dying of that situation. In adolescence there is a myth that semen is produced in such vast quantities that it needs to be discharged often so that it doesn't hurt from retention. That is a prayer that young males have: they want a biological sign that they need to have an orgasm so the tension will be reduced. They are actually deciding in their minds that the pressure is too much and something must be done about it, either find a mate or ejaculate some other way. Using women for sexual release is just plain selfishness. When you are not thinking about how someone feels or what your actions will initiate in the other person, then it is merely sensuality and lust. Many marriages are actually a legal permission slip to have sex, indulge in lusts and sensuality, without love or respect for each other.

We do not think of sex as dirty or sinful as long as it is done in the context of a responsible, responsive, thoughtful, loving, respectful and committed relationship. If you are shopping for a partner, we suggest you don't have sex until you get married. Sex is so powerful that it overwhelms other means of interacting. It is like blaring the stereo so loud on one channel that the other channels cannot be heard. Do not inject those intense feelings of sexual energy into a relationship until there is a loving container for those feelings to be held. The loving container can only be created if the two of you have spent time together talking and learning about each other and finding out if there is mutual respect and honoring of each other as individuals.

Do not work on more than one relationship at a time. If you have multiple partners, you will become confused because each person you have sex with creates a psychic tie with them that lasts nine months. During those nine months, if you have another partner, you will be picking up energy and feelings from both of them. You will start getting confused because you will have more than one person pulling and tugging at you and influencing you at the same time. They will in turn be picking up on your energies. If you are in a committed relationship, then you give all your attention to one person and receive all your attention from that person. Then you will know if the two of you are right for one another without a lot of extraneous influences. As the relationship tie develops over a period of time, a deeper love and trust develops and you will be able to know whether you want to spend your life with this person you love. It is a good idea at this point to set a date for the decision about whether to get married or not. Setting a date to set a date means that you are both not quite certain whether you are going to make this relationship a marriage, and you need something to goad you into finding out. The date you set is for you to decide to get engaged, and then decide on a marriage date not too distant in the future – or end the relationship. This puts the fire under both of you to either get it together or move on. On the other hand, if you are both sure about marriage, then just set the wedding date and get married.

In this world, we are so afraid of not being loved and cared for that we will do just about anything to make sure we acquire that love and care, by force if necessary. If you make a prayer for something, you will receive it. Leave the timing to God. Do not make the mistake of using a second relationship as leverage to measure the one you're in. Do not make the mistake of taking your frustrations out on your partner by starting another relationship before you have resolved the issues in the one you are in by dissolving it. That would be acting out of fear and pride: fear that you will never be taken care of the way you want, and pride that you should have just what you want, especially if no one will help you get what you want. Then you will just take it yourself. There is no trust in that approach. That is playing with the lives of others and causing them to feel insecure because you are not fully committed to the relationship you are in. Usually this is caused by some major dissatisfaction or anger in the relationship that you did not process and are not facing. We also fear being lonely and rush out to grab whatever we can. Some people will have a string of partners with nothing satisfying or spiritually fulfilling going on. Many times a spiritual need for connection with God is being masked by a conclusion that you need a man or woman to fulfill and complete you. Make sure you examine yourself to see if you actually have a spiritual need disguising itself as a way to keep from feeling lonely. You really need a relationship with God in order to feel whole and complete.

The way to regenerate in the physical body is to raise up the sexual energy into the heart and mind. The creative power of the energy used in sex will go to make you more whole, more loving, more patient and more aware. Even plants when they are pruned of their flowers and buds keep the seed within themselves and attain great strength and longevity. Many sexually indulgent people become emaciated as they waste the life force in selfishness. Passion has brought so much sorrow, suffering and sin into the world because it is using the creative power for sense gratification, whether with a partner or alone, and with or without a marriage contract. These sins of the flesh must be paid off in order for you to be free from them. Until you learn to subdue and control your passions, you will not experience true health. Instead of wasting your substance, refine and spiritualize your physical body by sending the creative fire upwards for regeneration. The less you allow your thoughts to go to sexual fantasies and sensual gratification, the purer your mind will be and you will be less led into those temptations. Let us respect the contract of marriage and hold to the idea that a committed, responsible relationship expresses perfect obedience and oneness with God. If the passions tempt you intensely, focus your mind, thought and imagination on something you desire to create: write a poem, play some music, paint a picture, work on some project or pray for a couple of people, and you will raise up that energy.

The process of transmutation of your energies will stimulate the regeneration, if you really want it to. Physical exercise accompanied with creative or spiritual thoughts is more effective than mere physical action alone. Meditation upon inspiring subjects has the power to transform forces, infusing the sexual fluids and uplifting them. By consciously directing pure love from the heart into the creative centers of the brain, sexual energies are changed and lifted up into spiritual energies. Every cell of the body can be made subject to your mental control. Patient persistence assures success. If you persist in raising these energies up you will experience better physical health, increased mental power, purer desires, and an unfoldment of innate spiritual qualities latent in every human being.

God created sex and saw that it was good. But human beings since the time of Adam and Eve have stepped outside the divine union and the experience of Eden. The first parents decided that the serpent force was interesting and indulged this interest in choosing between good and evil. Once this choice was made, Adam and Eve felt naked and exposed and felt an immediate difference between themselves and God. They clothed themselves because they felt shame for the first time because they had disobeyed the injunction of their Creator. They were forced to figure things out on their own and thrown out of Paradise. Childbirth was to be experienced with suffering until we could once again reconcile ourselves to our Creator. Human beings had adulterated the perfect relationship they had with God. The word "adultery" comes from the Latin root, "adulter" which means "one who approaches another unlawfully." To adulterate means to corrupt, pollute, to make impure by adding extra or improper ingredients. Adultery is completely unacceptable and sinful. It constitutes soul murder of spouse and children and moves you away from God.

It is for this reason that Jesus said that fornication causes others to commit adultery and is a justifiable reason for divorce. The word "fornicatus" is Latin for arch or vault. It comes from the etymological root "gwher" that means "warm." A "fornicatus" was a vaulted underground dwelling in Rome where poor people and prostitutes lived. It was a brothel and looked like a vaulted brick oven, so that's where we get our word "fornication." It means sexual intercourse between a man and a woman not married to each other. In Matthew 15:19, Jesus says, "For out of the heart proceeds evil thoughts, murders, adulteries, fornications, thefts, false witness and blasphemies." Fornication is the adulterating of a committed relationship with one's husband or wife. It creates a bond with a third party. This outside influence makes an added ingredient that contaminates the bond and confuses the tie between the husband and wife. This implies a strong disrespect and lack of love for the partner. Jesus said, "Whosoever looks on a woman to lust after her has committed adultery with her already in his heart" (Matthew 5:28). Here your body travels after the object of your desire. Whether you actually perform sexual intercourse or not, you have already done it in your mind.

Chapter Twenty Two

The Power of Sex

Why is a powerful attraction built into our sexual energies? Why do we get so excited by another person and have all those endorphins exploding in our bodies when we meet someone? That is the way God created us. We are supposed to feel all of those energies and life force flowing in our bodies so that here on earth, we find someone to share our lives with and raise our families.

Long before you have any idea what is happening to you, the hormones and glands release powerful chemicals into the bloodstream causing a revolution and unfolding of the reproductive energies. This happens at such a young age that it seems unfair or completely wrong, but it takes a number of years to fully develop into a biological adult. The physical body we are wearing is so magnificent, designed with such exquisite beauty and power, that only our Creator could have pictured it and fashioned it. Everything works the way it was created. The sexual energies start to rise and the reproductive part of our body undergoes drastic changes. The secondary male and female sexual characteristics respond producing hair growth and filling out. The curves of the body change, females developing lower body strength and males upper body strength.

Between the ages of 11 and 14 males and females will have some kind of awakening into sexual experience. Touching genitals begins to bring pleasure in ways not experienced before. It is natural and understandable that we explore these things and experience them. They are not bad or wrong. There is a right time and place for experiencing this with a loving and committed partner. It is always the thoughts and corresponding shame and guilt that make experiences like these ugly and dark. By teasing and shaming us, our friends add a dimension of contamination to what would be beautiful and wonderful. It is amazing that our bodies can feel the things they feel. It is awesome and incredible that such development and growth can occur in such a short time.

Females develop sexual characteristics earlier than males. As the breasts develop, girls become more self-conscious and aware of their gender. The ritual of shopping for a training bra becomes no small discussion for parents. Then there are discussions about makeup, pimples and dressing up. Boys watch girls develop with intense interest and a little fear. When boys and girls are 12 years of age, the girls are about two years ahead of boys in sexual and emotional de-

THE POWER OF SEX

velopment. At 15 the girls are only a year ahead of the boys. They catch up to each other emotionally in the middle of the sophomore year of high school, or 16 and a half.

When I was eleven and my sister was twelve, my mother took us to her room to explain the birds and the bees. I never understood how birds could be interested in bees, so it was confusing. What did birds do to bees? Did bees like birds? I never observed them together so it was very mysterious. But my mother, in her considerably repressed attempt to educate, told us a story of St. Maria Guerite who was 14 when she was viciously murdered. Apparently a 29-year-old man came up to her one day and demanded sex and she refused him. He had one of those hand scythes that cut tall grass and he hacked her up, stabbing her nineteen times and killed her. She died faithful to Jesus. Later, the Catholic Church canonized her a saint. That was my first talk on sex. I was not sure what sex was after this talk. I was terrorized and went away hoping that I would never turn 29 for fear that men became murderers because they want sex. I had had no awareness of sex up to that time. Then I thought maybe I should stay away from 14 year old girls. It was horrible. My mother did not mention love or relationship in that talk.

If you are lucky, your parents talked to you respectfully about love and sex. But I think most people did not get that information, except through friends or school. That is sad. I was fairly promiscuous as an adolescent and, like so many others, completely overwhelmed by sexual energies. I had no one to talk to about it and I explored this area quite a bit. I don't remember really getting to know the girls that I first had sexual experiences with. I don't think a person can know another person until they know themselves. I was emotionally lost and looking for a heart connection that would take the place of my loneliness. I think many of us have had similar experiences in adolescence. We are spiritually asleep at this age and lost to ourselves, hoping another person will comfort our confusion and melt away our sadness.

The whole world is lost in a sea of shame and guilt because as these sexual feelings are submerged and kept from the light of day, they cannot be aired out and cleared. You need to clear them and see them for what they are. They are powerful energies that cannot be taken lightly and should not be underestimated. They cannot be transformed and purified until they are aired out, talked about and released. I was a very passionate young male, lonely and afraid, like everyone else. I looked to the embrace of girls to steal love and affection.

It is said that the average adolescent male has a sexual thought every 20 seconds. That may be an exaggeration, but mostly true. The incredible power of the glandular explosion in the body reaches critical mass in early relationships. Hormones are causing major changes in the physical appearance and the reproductive organs come alive with sensitivity. Sex is one of the most physically reinforcing experiences people can have. The power of these feelings in the body, coupled with a conviction to abstain from intercourse, makes for an extremely volatile condition few have the strength to withstand. The conviction to wait until marriage usually caves in at some point because of how good sex feels in the body. Genital stimulation brings intense pleasure and if the moral judgments laid on people did not exist, there would be even less self-restraint, but also less guilt. It is very difficult to balance these energies in the body and get control of these forces. The guilt and shame that is put on people during their sexual awakening does not help anyone. On the other hand, indulging the feelings will not diminish them, but will in fact make them stronger. Any emotion or desire that you practice intensely and often will grow stronger. Expressing sexual feelings does not release them, but makes those feelings more likely to be expressed.

Girls feel sexual feelings as much as boys but place more importance on the closeness, safety, security and the feeling side of the relationship. When girls feel sexual feelings, they interpret those feelings as closeness. They sometimes think that if they allow sexual advances from boys, they will get the emotional feeling of closeness. Actual sexual intensity comes later for girls than for boys. Girls need to be taught not to allow boys to demand sex from them, waiting to get to know each other and learning to honor and respect one another. Since the likelihood of two people getting to know each other very well in adolescence is almost impossible, they should be waiting for a long time. We should teach girls the truth that boys seldom care personally about them, because the boys' understanding and sense of caring for another person in a relationship has not awakened yet. Sometimes, adult males can be as unrelated and disrespectful of the feelings of the woman as young males. Girls need to be taught that boys try to learn the right language to get what they want and that they are seldom sincere, as most boys are sexual opportunists and are looking for an experience and not a relationship.

Boys, on the other hand, want to make their mark sexually without regard to whether they feel close to the girl. They want sex without much concern for how the girl feels or what the nature of the relationship is. A few boys want to be close, but most boys want the experience of sexual intercourse or some sexually gratifying experience. Some boys earn social points from other boys if they go as far as they can with girls. It is a sign of prowess and success. Relationship is secondary. Boys will almost tolerate relationship with girls if they can have sexual intimacy. Younger boys, when confronted with the prospect of interacting with girls, would rather play video games and get involved in sports because girls are so mystifying and overwhelming to them. They have no clue about what emotional closeness or relatedness is about, much less have an inkling of real intimacy. It is an illusion to think that boys have any capacity for relatedness during adolescence. I am generalizing and of course, there are boys that have learned relatedness and want real intimacy. It is much rarer though.

Any touching that stimulates the genitals or causes arousal is sexual in nature. So any form of sex that touches or stimulates genitals is under the title "Having Sex" for purposes of this subject. These days, it is common for girls to be careless and opportunistic in sexual encounters in reaction to what boys and men have done for centuries. The girls are using the boys in the same way the boys used the girls in the past. There is no feeling and no concern for the effects of such action. The motivation is the stealing of a sensation of power, with no thought whatsoever for the object of their desire. The state of the world has degenerated so far as to numb out any feeling of concern for another human being's feelings.

Sexual energies are very difficult to manage once they have been experienced. It is incredible to imagine adolescents being able to control that energy. People experimenting sexually often feel that having intercourse is the next step in exploration of their sexual energies, but they have no idea of the feelings and changes that will occur in their bodies when they have sex early. They are not equipped to handle it emotionally. Yet adolescents want to feel grown up and do what adults do. Can you really blame them for trying to act like adults? Parents are expecting them to grow up and launch out into life and the freedom of college at 18.

A little known biological fact is that every night during sleep the blood flows into the penis and vagina in a regular cycle approximately every 45 minutes. The blood fills the penis and there is an erection. This happens to males from a few months old to above 80 years. This erection cycle is governed by the autonomic nervous system and it is nature's way of making sure the plumbing works to propagate the species. The vagina also flushes with blood on the same cycle and this is called tumescence. The uterus tilts forward, the labia swells and the vaginal walls lubricate. This phenomena is natural and of course, less visible than the erections that males wake up with. These cycles have nothing to do with sexual stimulation, erotic reading material or magazines and movies viewed the night before. It is God's way of making sure that human beings are able to procreate and make babies. Most boys feel that there is something wrong with them when they wake up with erections, and it would be good for them to know that this is a normal thing not related to sexual arousal or the beginning of becoming a sexual pervert or some sexual addict. On rare occasions there is a sexual dream that accompanies one of the erection or tumescent cycles and so people think that they are sexually out of control or assume that the cycle has to do with dreams. It mostly occurs without any dreams.

There is so much guilt put on people about sex, and yet our movies and TV are laden with implicit and explicit sexual content. Religion has tried to scare people away from sexually acting out with threats of eternal damnation. Because of the mixed messages from our culture and the powerful urges of the body, rules and regulations have not been very useful or effective in keeping young people from experimenting with sex. We recommend a general guideline that there should be no sexual intercourse until a young man or woman is mature enough and very sure that this person is the right person, and they want to build a committed relationship together in a holy marriage. They should wait until marriage for engaging in sex until they are sure that they are right for each other.

Most adults snicker and act like adolescents when it comes to sex. They still believe that there is something dirty, secret and dangerous about sex. Most of the world experiences sex as lust and sensuality. In fact, lust and sensuality completely ignore the partner and are really accomplished alone. Sensuality involves no one else and even if there is a willing or unwilling partner, there is no relatedness and very little respect involved. Any warm body will do, because it is about you and not about the potential oneness. It is not about respecting another human being, honoring their feelings or holding them in highest esteem. Sensuality is gratification of your appetites without consideration for the partner's feelings.

For most people, sex is dirty or unclean. This stems from past programming that females incite the males to lust, causing them to fall into temptation. Women have been the dumping ground of all the sexual woes of human beings. The Garden of Eden story explains Eve's mistake of being seduced by the serpent and she in turn making Adam fall. Well, Adam also chose and is equally responsible. The more afraid and shameful people get about sex, the more clandestine they become in their sexual practices. Sex is both feared and worshipped by millions of people. People indulge their lusts and conceal their shame about their sexual behavior.

Prohibitions about sex need to be worked through and discussed with your partner in order to be in a long-lasting and fulfilling relationship. For most people, your ideal mate is your fantasy of your ideal parent, the one you wanted your father or mother to be like. If the attachment to parents has not been too binding, and the relationship with the opposite sexed parent not excessively burdensome or painful, then a meaningful sexual relationship with a loved one can be developed.

We need to see our genitals with as much reverence as we do

our arms or head or hands. God created the whole body as good and that includes sex. It is the completion of the fullness of God, and in the act of sharing and bringing into balance the forces of creation we reflect God. In time, the gratification of personal and sexual needs in a relationship deepens and transforms into companionship and mutual emotional support. Sex can be an instrument of great joy and comfort to those who are truly joined together in a spiritual marriage. However, sex must not be the basis of a relationship. The movement of the spirit must be present following the commitment to God, Jesus and Mary.

Do you feel that the creation of your body in your mother's womb by the seed of your father was a degrading or dirty thing? You might say that your parents were married before God. We might ask you, "Were they?" Many people who are married are not spiritually married and do not have the level of respect and consideration that is required in a marriage blessed by God. They are married in the eyes of the world, but have not begun to understand spiritual union.

God, male and female is the eternal triangle. God must be the most important part of this triangle, or the relationship between man and woman will fail. It is necessary to have God in the triangle because that is the source of the power that allows the attraction, love and union in the first place. In order for a committed relationship between a man and a woman to work, you have to really know the complete function of God, man and woman. Only through this consciousness can you attain the balance of forces in your being. So what is this complete function of God? If you do not feel that God is real, then you would not be able to cooperate with God. If God set up the pattern of how relationships work and how power and love move between male and female, then you might want to know how that works in order to cooperate with it.

Sexual intercourse involves all the senses and feelings of the physical and spiritual bodies. Powerful energies are released and ignited in sexual affection. These energies are intoxicating and overwhelming if you do not know yourself very well, and can be damaging if you are only interested in your own gratification. There is a powerful heat given off when this combustion takes place. In fact, almost every time a person comes in contact with a person of the opposite gender, a tremor crosses the field of space as energy passes between you. This does not have to manifest in actually meeting or having sexual contact, but energy passes to and from two people, even if they never speak. What is going on here? God is the power and life that is in each of us and that energy rises up to greet the opposite, complementing it. Male and female are two distinct parts of the same energy, just like day and night, up and down, within and without. It is God meeting God, the energy of God in one person meeting the energy of God in another human being.

The physical sexual act is only the visible manifestation of a spiritual reality taking place. Most people see only the appearances and the outer actions and refuse to acknowledge what is taking place in the spiritual body or in their feelings. The power of sex expresses through the glands and hormones of the body pulsing with force and power. The glands are the points in the body where emotions are generated and vibrations released. This pulsing of energy is the giving or accepting of love. It is God giving and receiving to God through the male and female human body.

During periods of intense spiritual growth when you are being prepared for illumination, Self-realization or ordination, it may be necessary for you to abstain from sexual relations so that the power and energy may help to bring about changes in your physical body. After you attain a certain degree of spiritual attainment and the light of Christ in your body, you would harm a person who is not on the spiritual path by having sexual relations with them. It would leave an imprint on them that no one else would be able to satisfy.

> Surely you know your bodies are part of Christ himself? So I must never take the parts of Christ and join them to a prostitute! It is written, "The two will become one flesh." So you should know that anyone who joins with a prostitute becomes one flesh with the prostitute. But the one who joins with the Lord is

one spirit with the Lord. So flee from sexual immorality. Every other sin people do is outside their bodies, but those who sin sexually sin against their own bodies. You should know that your body is a temple for the Holy Spirit who is in you, which you have of God, and you are not your own. For you were bought with a price. So glorify God in your body and in your spirit, which are God's (I Corinthians 6:15).

Chapter Twenty Three

Spiritual Marriage

Imagine a world where human beings are not permitted to marry unless they know themselves. If you knew yourself well, you would know your strengths and weaknesses. You would know what your gifts and talents are because you would see them already expressing through you. You would have love for yourself and be confident that your nature was fine the way it is. You would not necessarily need anybody to be your companion. You would not feel that you were nothing without someone else or that you were so incomplete that you had to have someone in your life in order to feel whole. You would not desire someone to provide you with strengths you do not have or shore you up in areas you feel you are lacking. Your loneliness would not drive you to connect with people out of inner insecurity. You would not be lonely because you would be conscious that you have God inside you. You would not connect out of neediness, but you would only connect with others because your nature is one of radiant love and giving.

In reality, you are drawn to a partner because you see in the other the reflection of yourself. In the beginning God set it up as a cosmic pattern that opposites would bond with each other and become one flesh. In the material world, this pattern is necessary in order to propagate the human species. If there were nothing to attract you, then you would not be drawn to your partner. So you seek out a partner, a mate or companion because they are going to add a dimension of relationship and experience that the two of you together will share. This sharing is not out of neediness, but because the fullness of the experience that you will share together brings greater depth and love to both of you.

Peace between male and female can only exist if you really understand the way God works. Male and female are two energies, each containing the quieter nature of the other, while manifesting the complementary energies of each other. This is the way God set it up and we cannot change it. The idea that we could dominate, control or otherwise possess another is against God's basic pattern and will always lead to conflict. Male and female must complement and balance each other because they are both interdependent and must work together to experience a full and balanced life. Each of us is complete within ourselves, having a soul personality and a Self that is God. The Self does not need anything. The soul may need to grow, expand, express and experience many things, while the Self is whole and complete within you. The soul is your personality and experience, while the Self is the part of you that is God: infinite, powerful and radiant Light.

When two people say they love each other, they are saying that they feel the power and force of God moving through them trying to pass from one to the other. This is the power of God, and demonstrates the wonders of this glorious creation that God created. When two people accept love from each other they are reflecting the Heavenly pattern which is wonderful, beautiful and ecstatic. The power of God moves across the waters of our human lives and touches through our soul onto the shore of our physical existence. This power thrills the emotional body and intensely exhilarates our feelings. The body ignites with energy and excitement in the intense experience of love. The touch, the caress, the acceptance and respect as the eyes meet, the engulfing ebb and flow, inexpressible and uncontrollable, this is God moving across the great ocean of sex in the embrace of two lovers. In this turbulent, wonderful containment and penetration there bursts forth the million seed-like human forms contained within each person, the very mirror of the creativity of the being in whom we live and move. This is the pattern the Creator visualized and pronounced by the word when the worlds were formed. And God said that it was good.

The sacred temple, our physical body, encloses a most powerful life force. It has the ability to make bodies like itself, through procreation, propagating other human beings all over the earth. The mind of God holds the pattern and possibility of our incarnation through the love of a man and a woman. When two people know this connection, this love, they will feel and identify with the one reality within. They will begin to know and understand love as a divine pattern. Love between two people causes a stirring of the soul and begins the process of waking up. When powerful feelings and emotions wash over you like a tidal wave, either in great suffering, great love or ecstatic union, your soul begins to wake up to God's divinity within you.

Love is only attained between two people when the male declares his love for the woman. He then lets her go, setting her free and giving her up to the God she represents and waits for her to come to him. In the animal kingdom this is the usual pattern. From an electrical standpoint, the negative wire, the female, always flows to the positive, male. If it works this way in the physical world, it works this way in the spiritual world. When the male declares his love and his intentions, he has made a pattern and started the movement of energy between them. The man and woman must meet in one heart and the one mind of God, through which all energy passes.

A good way to describe this process is using the infinity symbol. Place the infinity symbol or the figure eight on its side. As the energy moves, flowing over the right hand loop, that is the male stating his love for the female. As the two loops intersect, the sexual union occurs where he gives his power to the female body. She takes in this power through the sexual embrace. But she takes in much more than that. She takes in the energies representing the state of his respect and acceptance of her, the energy of his mind, his thoughts, feelings and the state of his consciousness. She takes in where he is emotionally and what he is confused by. She takes in the whole gamut of where he is, as well as the seed or sperm, which carry the energies of his blood, and the powerful energies that go to empower her body. Much more is going on here than just the physical. It is mostly spiritual energies that are being transferred. As we continue the movement on the figure eight, the energy passes into the female body and she works on those energies in the dark and in the quiet. She does not know at first what is happening inside of her. If there is a baby created, then the energies will become organic, hormonal, emotional and physical. If no baby is conceived, then that energy will be processing and sorting within her for a few days or maybe a week as the energy moves up into her conscious awareness. This is shown in the movement to the upper portion on the female side of the figure eight. At this point she becomes conscious of what he gave her. She feels all of the emotions, feelings, power, clarity and confusion of his energy and she now is beginning to understand it and has things to say to him about it. She wants to give back to him in the flow of energy something of what he gave her, only it will be given back in a form raised up from what it was.

The nature of the feminine is to take in energy, work on it for a little while and then give it back in a transformed and raised up condition. She feels the need to share this with him and this is the point of intersection on the downward spiral. Often, the man will say that he is closed for business and does not want to receive. He feels his job is to give and she should receive. If he shuts down her reflections a number of times, then she will start having more difficult menstrual cycles or painful periods. The more backlogged she gets with her feelings, the more the two avoid resolving issues that are coming up in the relationship, the more he is resisting his own growth and learning in the relationship. Then she will stop receiving him sexually because he is cutting the cycle and refusing the transformation that her natural energies could provide to the relationship.

If the male receives her loving energies of what he gave her, he will grow and as he receives from her, the energy moves down the figure eight on his side and raises him up to a more sensitive, aware and responsive level as the relationship develops. This is a very powerful experience and takes some faith and trust to allow another person to mirror things and show things to us. We have to love and get ourselves out of the way quite a bit to let this happen. Then the spiral continues as the male becomes clearer and his energies in the ocean of sex are more truly loving and open.

In the beginning of creation, male and female were not separated into polar opposites, but were in one body. It was androgynous and a human being could propagate from itself. When the genders were separated, the male gave the female the love aspect and this is what she must give back to the male in relationship. It is a spiritual transfer that takes place in the sexual union. The male gives the female the power to care for and guide another being. If there is no child born, it gives power to the female body. She can convert this power into creativity of mind. Without this power given to her, she would not be able to have much effect on the world around her. She would lack the decisive quality of knowingness and authority.

The masculine energy gives the female the aspect of decision and knowing of choice. This is authority and the ability to discriminate between things that are good and things that are not good. The female gives the male the softness of touch, both physically and through the word and use of sound in communication. The protection for children against danger, the energies of healing, the ability to be present in the here and now, and the ability to connect in a related way are all energies contained in the female aspect. If a woman does not have the masculine aspect, she is unable to know what she wants and has trouble making decisions. She has trouble choosing. She may be self-centered and envious, not sure of her own authority in the world. If a man does not have the feminine aspect, he can be severe, cold and lacking in sensitivity, friendship or appreciation for beauty and art. He will lack kindness and tact and will be unable to be present in the here and now. His relationship skills will be undeveloped.

The feminine aspect in both men and women provides healing for everyone, through teaching parents about children, the philosophy and science of life as well as respect and consideration for other people. It has been said that women could stop all wars because she is able to instill peace in her partner. If all the women of the world would say no more sex if the males go off to war, then there would be no war or very short wars. When the female turns her head up to the male, she is accepting the spiritual aspect of the male. Whether the cycle is completed in the physical or not, she has opened the way for the activation of the life force in order to make it possible for the two to become one. Their energies must resonate in order for the cycle to be completed. If the male takes the female in his arms, he becomes the power that flows into her and he must give everything of himself to her in order to reach his own fulfillment. If the female is afraid of the male, she should stay away from him because she will not be able to let go in the embrace. Our bodies do not lie and we cannot fake openness. If you don't love him and love to be touched by him, then something is wrong. If you do not like the way he smells, then the relationship will not grow into very much. Something may need to be resolved or you might be with the wrong person.

What people don't realize is that the female gains her power and freedom in the sexual union, if the relationship is a committed and respectful relationship. Women sometimes have the mass-mind opinion that she is bestowing some kind of favor on the male through having sex with him. This is a misconception and presupposes that she is using sex to control the male until her ego is satisfied. She will try to obsess him with sexual energies, teasing and controlling by granting or refusing favors, until he reaches the limits of his tolerance and rebels against her refusals. Then sex becomes an economy where power is the currency and true intimacy cannot be experienced. The economy of sex means that sexual favors or the sexual experience are exchanged for something else. Having sex with your partner so he or she won't get in a bad mood is one example. Using sex to get an okay on a major purchase is another example. When there are fears of closeness in a relationship, other unresolved issues besides sex need to be addressed and cleared before expecting to share sexually.

Opposite polarities attract one another and it is the nature of flesh bodies to do this. There is life force passing between people all the time. In the initial stages of dating or courting, it is nearly impossible to ignore the life force moving between two people. There is usually some sexual arousal and attraction at first. The longing for love from another person is really the longing for God's love. When we love someone, we actually love the Godlike qualities that we glimpse more perfectly in the other person. However, even the most precious person can express only a portion of such perfection, for they are not Love itself. They will always fall short of the perfection of God. So seek at the source for true love. We seek love from each other because it is the nearest approach to heaven we know. As long as we put too much faith and dependency on people and things, they will likely fail us or be taken from us. The best place for our total reliance is on God. Only God is changeless, ever present infinite, ever available and always perfect love.

Most people seek a partner when they feel some sexual desire and they spend the rest of the time removing from the relationship all traces of intimacy and closeness. Libra is the astrological sign of marriage and relationship. It is the sign of crucifixion through relationship because you are giving up your sense of "me" and starting to consider the sense of "we." In order to receive, you must first give. If you are trying to channel everything to yourself, you will not be giving and you will stop receiving. Selfishness is the best way to stop relating and start just co-existing.

Marriage can be defined simply as the bringing together and bonding of two opposite but complimentary aspects for the purpose of bringing about a new creation. Marriage is the union of two distinct elements. Marriage is not a concept, a piece of paper or an event. All of these bring into tangible manifestation the commitment two people make in the process of getting married. Marriage is a living entity that results from the combination and blending of lives, aspirations and experiences of two different people, a man and a woman. Each person contributes the essence of their nature in order to form a completely new substance. In the sharing of their lives the two form a bond that ties the spiritual bodies together over time. This is so real and tangible that it becomes the means of their unity and the way they communicate their experiences. "And the two shall become one flesh."

In the Order of Christ Sophia, we state very clearly in our marriage sacrament that God is to be the first party of the marriage. In the past, if a person wanted to serve God, they became a monk or a nun and entered a monastery or convent. Marriage was considered to be for people who didn't have a full calling to serve God or who didn't have enough faith or conviction to sacrifice all for God. In this Aquarian Age, marriage is the foundation of Christian life. We recognize and teach marriage as a divine vocation, with as much integrity and sacramental purpose as living a celibate life in a monastery. Marriage is a school designed for spiritual liberation. Each person in the marriage provides a reflective substance that allows the other to see oneself. The trinity of knowing God, knowing oneself and knowing another applies very well to marriage.

Marriage between two people who are seeking God and trying to follow God's direction in their lives makes for a life on the razor's edge. There is no quiet place to hide or run away. It is a life continuously propelled into confrontation with your own inner nature and with the personality and idiosyncrasies of your partner. Learning to communicate effectively is especially important so that your egos do not run into conflict and you do not hurt each other too much. It is your different personalities and different upbringing that presents the greatest challenges in marriage. There will always be differences, especially when you consider the vast amount of experience each person brings with them from many lifetimes. How both of you deal with these differences determines whether your relationship will cramp and paralyze you, or grow and deepen you.

Chapter Twenty Four

Love as Ecstasy

"There can be no greater love for the Lord and for our neighbour than this ability to suffer and die to give glory to the Lord and eternal salvation to our brothers. To save ourselves for our own sake? It is very little. It is the 'least' degree of holiness. It is beautiful to save other people, by sacrificing ourselves, to love to such an extent as to become a sacrificing fire to save our neighbour. Love is then perfect. And great will be the holiness of such generous souls" (*The Poem of the Man-God*, Vol. 3, p. 610-611).

Being in God is not hard. It is the only peace you will ever know. Letting God love you is not dangerous or scary. It is the most bliss you will ever experience. Giving over everything to God will not destroy you, but the best parts of you will rise like a new sprout in springtime dancing in the radiance of the sun, rejoicing that life is moving and God is good. The part of you that is God, the Self, is waiting for what your outer person thinks of you to relax and give over the control and direction of your life to God. When you do that, and you must want that in order to do it, then God will remodel your whole life. God will refashion you in God's image and likeness and all parts of you will reflect God's wishes. Finally, God will be able to use you because there will be no part that is afraid. You cannot fear when you feel God's love. It is impossible.

In *The Poem of the Man-God*, Vol. 3, Jesus says:

"My doctrine is perfection. It is refinement of feelings and judgment....And I tell you that aversion, detachment and indifference are already hatred. Simply because they are not love. Hatred is the opposite of love. Can you find another name for aversion? For being detached from a being? For indifference? He who loves has a liking for the person loved. So if he dislikes him, he no longer loves him. He who loves, even if he is separated materially from the person he loves, continues to be near him with his spirit. So if one is detached with one's spirit from the other, one no longer loves the other. He who loves is never indifferent towards the person he loves, on the contrary he is interested in everything concerning that person. So if one is indifferent towards another, it means the one does not love the other. You can thus see that those three attitudes are branches of one plant: hatred. Now what happens when we are offended by one whom we love? In ninety per cent of the cases, if hatred does not arise, aversion, detachment or indifference will result. No. Do not do that. Do not freeze your hearts by means of those three forms of hatred. Love.

But you are asking yourselves: 'How can we?' I reply to you: 'As God can, as He loves those who offend Him.' A sorrowful but still good love. You say: 'How do we do that?' I am giving a new law on the relationship with a guilty brother or sister, and I say: 'If your brother offends you, do not humiliate him by reproaching them in public, but urge your love to cover up your brother's fault in the eyes of the world.' Because great will be your merit in the eyes of God, by barring, out of love, every satisfaction to your pride.

Oh! How people love to let people know that they were offended and grieved thereby. Like a foolish beggar they do not go to a king asking for alms in gold, but they go to other foolish beggars like themselves asking for handfuls of ash and manure and mouthfuls of burning poison. That is what the world gives to the offended person who goes complaining and begging comfort. God, the King, gives pure gold to him, who, being offended, goes without any grudge to weep only at His feet and ask Him, Love and Wisdom, for comfort of love and how to behave in the sorrowful circumstance. Therefore, if you want comfort, go to God and act with love.

I say to you, correcting the old law: 'If your brother has sinned against you, go and correct him by yourself. If he listens to you, you have gained your brother once again. And at the same time you have gained many blessings from God. If your brother does not listen to you, but he rejects you persisting in his fault, take with you two or three grave, clever, reliable witnesses, so that no one may say that you are agreeable to his fault or indifferent to the welfare of his soul, and go back to your brother with them, and kindly repeat your remarks in their presence, so that the witnesses may be able to repeat that you have done everything in your power to correct your brother in a holy way. Because that is the duty of a good brother, since the sin committed by him against you is detrimental to his soul, and you must take care of his soul. If that is of no avail, inform the synagogue, so that he may be called to order in the name of God. If even so he does not make amends and he rejects the synagogue or the Temple as he rejected you, consider him as a publican and a Gentile.

Do that both with your full brothers and with the people you love" (p. 18-19).

The fact that you care about other people should make you love more perfectly those who have been reborn in grace. There is a grace that showers down from the Creator on all those who give themselves over to God and let God love them. God wants everyone to open to let this happen. God loves everyone with a perfect and powerful love and no one is left out of that blessing. The ones who open to that love are the ones who are filled with the ecstasy of love. They know they are completely held and contained in the embrace of God as a conscious, divine being. You must love your neighbor as yourself. Everyone is your neighbor and so you must love each person in the whole world just the same way you love God and God loves everyone. Love thinks good thoughts about other people. Love supports and is kind. Love rejoices in the successes of other people. Love understands and feels empathy for another person's pain. Love gives. Love encourages and forgives because you remember that except for God's grace, you could have made the same mistake someone else has made. In fact, if you have a very good memory, you recollect clearly having made the very same mistake many times in the past and can easily have compassion for others because you know what making that same mistake feels like and the results of it. Be patient and slow to react with everyone.

You start out on the path like a new child in Christ, barely able to hold your head up. When you really see your errors and sins, you feel ashamed and painfully aware of how far you have to go to be close to God. Then you won't scandalize anyone else for their faults because you were in their shoes only moments ago, and need to apply the same loving acceptance for them that is given to you as a new child in Christ. In a few blinks of an eye, those errors and misconceptions are washed off of you by a few communions and blessings. So it can all change, and nothing will remain the same as it was yesterday. Get used to the powerful movement of the grace of God in your life.

God's grace is a movement of spirit and ecstatic containment in the Presence of God. No fear is possible there. No traces of pride can stand to stay where God's love resides. All the future possibilities of union with the divine open themselves before you as you give over more and more into the love of God.

"Give your relatives means of subsistence as compensation for your abandoning the house to follow Me, because it is unfair to deprive children and wife of their daily bread. And if you cannot sacrifice money, sacrifice the wealth of your affections. They are money which God evaluates for what they are: gold which is purer than any other gold; pearls which are more precious than those taken from the sea, and rubies which are rarer than those found in the bowels of the earth. Because to renounce one's family for My sake

is love which is more perfect than the purest gold, it
is a pearl made of tears, a ruby made of blood wailing
from the wound of one's heart, torn to pieces by the
separation from father and mother, wife and children.
But such purses never wear out, such treasures never
fail. Thieves cannot break into Heaven. Wood-worms
cannot eat what is deposited there. And have Heaven
in your hearts and your hearts in Heaven near your
treasures. Because a heart, whether good or wicked,
is with what you consider your dear treasure. So as a
heart is there where its treasure is (in Heaven), so the
treasure is there where the heart is (within you), nay,
the treasure is within the heart and with the treasure
of saints, in the heart there is the Heaven of saints."
(*The Poem of the Man-God*, Vol. 3, p. 12-13).

"It is the first commandment: Love and love. He who
does not love lies in professing to be a Christian. It is
useless to frequent the Sacraments and rites, it is useless to pray if one lacks charity. They become formulae
and even sacrileges" (*The Poem of the Man-God*, Vol.
3, p. 131).

In *The Poem of the Man-God*, Vol. 3, p. 160-161, Jesus is
speaking to the boy Marjiam about his future priesthood
and consoling him because both his parents were killed by a

mean man:

"Souls are like birds, enclosed in the cages of bodies. The earth is the place where they are brought with their cages. But they yearn for the freedom of Heaven: for the Sun which is God; for Nourishment suitable to them, which is the contemplation of God. No human love, not even the holy love of a mother for her children or of children for their mother, is so strong as to suffocate such yearning of souls to be rejoined to their Origin, which is God. Likewise God, because of His perfect love for us, finds no reason so strong as to exceed His desire to be rejoined to the soul longing for Him. What happens then? Sometimes He loves it so much that He says to it: 'Come, I will free you.' And He says so even if there are some children around a mother. He sees everything. He knows everything. What He does, He does well. When He frees a soul – the limited intelligence of men may not think so, but it is true – when He frees a soul, He always does it for a greater welfare of the soul itself and of its relatives. As I have already told you, He then adds to the ministry of the guardian angel the ministry of the soul which He has called to Himself, and which loves its relatives with a love free from human burdens, because it loves them in God. When He frees a soul, He binds Himself to take its place in taking care of the survivors. Has He not done that with you? Has He not made you, little child of Israel, My disciple, My future priest?"

"I will tell you also, what I told My little disciple. The Kingdom belongs to the faithful lambs who love and follow Me without getting lost in allurements. They love Me till the end" (*The Poem of the Man-God*, Vol. 3, p. 433).

"Do you know how a person can possess infinite love? By being so united to God, as to be all one with God. Then, as the creature disappears in the Creator, it is the Creator Who really acts, and He is infinite. And My apostles must be like that, all one with their God through the power of love, which is so close to the Origin as to dissolve in it. It is not the way in which you speak, but the way in which you love, that will convert hearts. Will you find sinners? Love them. Will you suffer because of disciples who go astray? Try to save them through love" (*The Poem of the Man-God*, Vol. 3, p. 635).

About the Author

Father Peter Bowes is a Priest and Master Teacher in the mystical Christian Order of Christ Sophia. He has been teaching and training people on the spiritual path, bringing the inner teachings of Jesus and Mary to those seeking real connection to God. Prior to co-directing the Order of Christ Sophia, Father Peter received his Masters and Doctoral degrees in Educational Psychology and ran his own practice for 20 years. He is the author of *The Word Within*, *Spiritual Astrology* , *Steps on the Way*, and *The Radical Path*, all of which possess his characteristic wisdom and authority. He lives in Chicago and travels frequently to give spiritual seminars all over the country.

For more information about Father Peter, please visit:
FatherPeter.CentersOfLight.org or
www.FatherPeterBowes.com